Innovative Technology in Art Conservation

Innovative Technology in Art Conservation provides one of the first ever critical assessments of innovation in conservation science and questions what role it should play in conservation and conservation ethics.

Written in language understandable for the non-technical reader, the book begins with a brief history of so-called science-based conservation, examining how it developed based on the history of codes of conservation ethics and conservation decision-making. It takes a critical look at so-called innovative technologies in art conservation and what such technologies are actually offering to the field. As an example, the results of advanced technologies for the high-resolution digital documentation and reproduction of works of art are examined in light of the concept of original appearance and perception science, how people see and perceive objects. The book concludes with some reflections on the future of science-based conservation, calling for more thoughtful consideration of what it is that is being offered, and why and for whom.

Innovative Technology in Art Conservation is essential reading for the international community of conservators, heritage professionals who must make decisions about the use of advanced technologies in conservation and conservation science, as well as important reading for academics and students.

Dr. W. (Bill) Wei (1955) is a retired senior conservation scientist in the Research Department of the Cultural Heritage Agency of the Netherlands (RCE – Rijksdienst voor het Cultureel Erfgoed), and now an independent consultant. He has a B.S.E. in mechanical engineering from Princeton University (1977) and a Ph.D. in materials science from the University of Illinois at Urbana-Champaign (1983). Before working in the cultural heritage field, he spent almost 20 years in industrial research and development in the areas of advanced materials, mechanical properties, and corrosion. He has been conducting research into and consulting with conservators for over 25 years on the effects of cleaning, treatments, and vibrations on the appearance and perception of objects of art cultural heritage. Dr. W. (Bill) Wei has trained as a Socratic dialogue moderator and has organized and moderated over 50 dialogues in the past ten years to help museums and conservation professionals understand each other's and their own views on controversial issues in conservation ethics.

Conservation in Focus

Innovative Technology in Art Conservation
Original Appearance and Viewer Perception
Dr. W. (Bill) Wei

Innovative Technology in Art Conservation

Original Appearance and Viewer Perception

Dr. W. (Bill) Wei

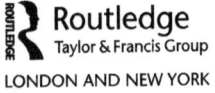
Routledge
Taylor & Francis Group

LONDON AND NEW YORK

First published 2024
by Routledge
4 Park Square, Milton Park, Abingdon, Oxon OX14 4RN

and by Routledge
605 Third Avenue, New York, NY 10158

Routledge is an imprint of the Taylor & Francis Group, an informa business

© 2024 William Wei

British Library Cataloguing-in-Publication Data
A catalogue record for this book is available from the British Library

ISBN: 978-1-032-10937-4 (hbk)
ISBN: 978-1-032-10939-8 (pbk)
ISBN: 978-1-003-21780-0 (ebk)

DOI: 10.4324/9781003217800

Typeset in Times New Roman
by Apex CoVantage, LLC

The colored figures can be accessed via the online Routledge Resource Centre www.routledge.com/9781032109374

Contents

The colored figures can be accessed via the online Routledge Resource Centre
www.routledge.com/9781032109374

Preface

What did a work of art or, for that matter, a historical object originally look like? This is one of the most fundamental and challenging questions that lies behind decisions that cultural heritage professionals – in particular, conservators – must make on how an object should be preserved for future generations. For many objects, the original appearance is tightly interwoven with their original function and their eventual place in history. It is therefore not surprising that decisions about how an object should be treated continue to be the subject of vigorous debate among collectors, conservators, curators, historians, museum directors, and the viewing public. The ultimate dream is if one cannot bring a work of art back to its original appearance, they can at least provide a visualization of how it originally appeared.

Roughly since the so-called cleaning controversy at the National Gallery of London after World War II, the cultural heritage profession has increasingly looked to the natural sciences and engineering for "objective" support in the debate surrounding what many now admit are "subjective" conservation decisions. Since then, what is now known as science-based conservation has left an indelible mark on how objects are analyzed, safely treated, and restored.

This apparent success has created an almost insatiable appetite in the conservation and conservation science world for the further development of so-called advanced and innovative technologies so that works of art can be examined at (digital) resolutions down to atomic levels. With such precise information, it is believed, or at least hoped, that one can eventually determine what the works originally looked like and, even better, preserve them, as the adage goes, for the enjoyment, education, and memory of future generations. However, this begs the question as to whether this confidence in advanced and innovative technology is justifiable for the practical world of art conservation.

This book takes a critical look at the continued development and use of so-called innovative technologies, which are thought to provide "objective" evidence for the determination of the original appearance of objects of art and cultural heritage, something that, in fact, depends on viewer perception and context, and is thus "subjective" in nature. Written in language understandable for the non-technical reader, it begins with a brief history of science-based conservation, that is, based on the "hard sciences" of chemistry, physics, and engineering, and how it developed from a perceived need for an objective basis for conservation codes of ethics and conservation decision-making. The book then considers the concepts of originality, original appearance, and the "soft science" of perception, and how people see and perceive such objects. With this background, the book focuses on advanced technologies such as color modeling, hyperspectral imaging, virtual retouching and digital reproductions, and texture mapping. These technologies are critically examined in terms of what they offer for determining original appearance, as opposed to what heritage professionals and the general public can actually see and perceive. In fact, it is postulated that while such innovative developments have improved conservation decision-making, they have gone too far, creating a new reality in how people see and perceive works of art. It is questionable whether that is desirable. It is recommended that more thoughtful consideration be given to the question as to what it is that conservation scientists with their advanced equipment are offering, and why and for whom it is being offered.

This book is not a critical review of the literature on the aforementioned fields, a review or reviews of which could be the topic of several books. As the conservation and conservation science fields are wont to say, this book takes a multidisciplinary or, rather, interdisciplinary look at current developments in the conservation science field. The intended audience is quite broad, including professionals with a limited technical background. In many cases, many of the technologies are thus explained in simpler terms than usual. The examples include work that I have come in contact with in one way or another in over 25 years in the conservation and conservation science field, work that I conducted while at the Cultural Heritage Laboratory of the Cultural Heritage Agency of the Netherlands, Amsterdam. Although the book concentrates on objects of visual art, the message of this book applies for the role of innovation and advanced technologies in all fields of the conservation of cultural heritage.

There are a number of people to whom I owe great thanks for the writing of this book. First, thanks go to the editor, Heidi Lowther of Routledge Books, who originally contacted me about writing a book based on a talk I once gave on eye-tracking, an innovative technology that I was not qualified to write about as a stand-alone subject. However, she was quite enthusiastic about this broader view of a conservation scientist of my own field and colleagues. I would also like to thank my former colleague, IJsbrand Hummelen, paintings conservator and research scientist at the Cultural Heritage Agency of the Netherlands, for introducing me to the complexities of conservation ethics, and the love-hate relationship between conservation and conservation science. I would also like to thank my former colleague, Karen ter Brake-Baldock of the Cultural Heritage Agency of the Netherlands, as well as Natasha Herman, private book conservator, and Rebecca Rushfeld, private textile conservator and consultant, for reading the first drafts of this book. Though they may not agree with all of my arguments, their critical questions and comments have greatly helped to clarify the text. Above all, I would like to thank my wife, Ida van der Lee, community and ritual artist, for her love and support during the writing of this book, as well as countless other projects which this busy-holic (not just work) has had at the same time.

1 Introduction – conservation science and conservation ethics

The discussion in this book revolves around the role that conservation science – in particular, innovative technologies – plays in the conservation of works of visual art. This chapter briefly sets the stage for this discussion. The chapter first looks at what conservation of visual art and, for that matter, cultural heritage entails. A brief history of the conservation field is then reviewed. In particular, the development of strict interpretations of professional codes of ethics and the resulting fear of failure are considered, both of which have led, in part, to the development of the modern field of conservation science. Finally, developments in conservation science are briefly reviewed in order to bring the reader up to the point where innovative technologies in conservation can be considered.

1.1 Originality and art conservation

What is visual art? On the one hand, this may seem like a silly question. One might simply say that it is any work of art object that can be seen. On the other hand, the question is one of a subset of questions related to the philosophical question of what art itself is. For the purposes of this book, the term "visual art" refers to objects that are made to somehow communicate with viewers through their eyes as sensors and their brains as some sort of interpreter. Although there is overlap, this definition is also used to distinguish it from such forms of art as literature and the performing arts such as dance, music, and theater. Simply said, the term "visual art" as used in this book refers to objects that people look at, perceive, and interpret. Whether an object can actually be considered art or not is beyond the scope of this book.

Works of art can be found in two-dimensional form, such as drawings and lithographs, paintings, photographs or tapestries, and three-dimensional form, such as applied art and design, carvings, figurines and statues, and electronic form. Architecture is also considered by many to be a form of three-dimensional visual art, and the interiors of such works can also contain works of art including wall paintings, figurines, and other decorative features that are permanently installed. The definition of two- and three-dimensionality

DOI: 10.4324/9781003217800-1

is not strict. It can be argued that paintings with impasto (thick paintbrush strokes) and many contemporary multi-media works of art also have a strong three-dimensional character even though they are displayed in nominally two-dimensional frames.

Works of art are considered by their owners to have some sort of importance, meaning, significance, or value. These can be described, for example, as cultural, economic, aesthetic, emotional, or historical. People often try to draw meaning from a work of art by trying to understand the artist's intent. The artist supposedly has made the work for some reason. The work of art may tell a story, historical or otherwise, or convey a message, or it can be just viewed and/or enjoyed for what it is. It may be an example of "good" art or something produced by a "good," "well-known" artist and thus have high commercial and cultural/societal value.

Note that many objects from so-called third world countries or other cultures are considered works of art by the Western industrialized world. However, they are actually ritual objects, valuable in their own right, which were originally endowed by their makers with some sort of religious or traditional symbolic meaning. These include objects ranging from the world's largest religions to objects used in local cultural traditions.

As works of art grow older, their material condition changes chemically and physically. In most cases, these often-gradual changes result in concomitant gradual changes in the appearance of the works. At some point in time, many, but not all, owners or custodians of the objects begin to feel the need to somehow slow down, stop, or undo this so-called aging process. There is thus a growing urge to preserve these works, pretty much for the same reason that people want to preserve objects of cultural heritage in general. As the saying goes, works of art should be preserved in order to pass them on to future generations, so that they can also enjoy, value, and learn from those works. It is noted that this perceived need to deal with the aging process is a Western approach to dealing with works of art or works from other cultures collected by citizens of Western industrialized nations and considered to be art in the Western sense (see previous paragraph). Whether the original cultures would see the need to preserve such objects in the context of their original ritual functions is an important discussion, which is, however, beyond the scope of this book.

In order to preserve a work of art, it is often brought to someone known as an art conservator, someone trained and qualified to analyze and treat (or not) that particular type of work. What constitutes sufficient training and qualifications is an ongoing subject of often heated debate in the international art and heritage conservation profession, a debate which also is not within the scope of this book.[1] It is, however, generally recognized in the cultural heritage field that a trained and qualified art conservator will have sufficient knowledge about the particular types of works he or she is working on, including art history, the materials, and how the artist worked, and have sufficient practical skills to perform the necessary treatments or implement the necessary preventive conservation measures.

The art conservator first analyses the object, determining its current physical and chemical state, and conducts research into the history of the object, the context in which it was made, and the artist's technique and way of thinking, that is, the artist's intent. The conservator must then decide among a number of possible treatments for the object. These can include actual chemical and/ or physical treatments of the object, so-called active conservation, to achieve a desired result. However, the possibilities also include not doing anything to the object and resorting to recommending exhibition and storage conditions that can slow the aging process down, so-called preventive conservation. The reader may, for example, be familiar with the climate and lighting controls used by museums to slow down the aging process of particular types of objects.

The critical issue behind decisions in the conservation of art, and one of the main drivers for innovative technology in art conservation, lies in the innocent phrase "to achieve a desired result." What a desired result should be, or the other way around, what it may not be, continues to be a subject of often heated debate in the cultural heritage community.

If one were to ask a layperson about what they would expect from the conservation of a work of art, one may receive an answer such as the work of art should be made to be like new again or as good as new, or it should be treated so that it is as original or authentic as possible. However, if one were to ask heritage professionals, one would probably receive an extensive discussion and/or a heated debate about the following possibilities and all of the gradations in between. Bring the object

- back to a condition as close to the original state as possible
- back to some state close to the original state as safely as possible
- back to one of the important layers of its history while retaining evidence of the other layers
- to an authentic state, and/or
- some stable condition which maintains the work's integrity and respects the artist's intentions.

It is highly likely that the option of leaving the work of art in its current state and taking preventive conservation measures would also be included in the professional discussion. Once a treatment decision has been made and carried out, the debate often continues in terms of whether the result was good or not.

The literature on the conservation of art is replete with opinions, often outspoken and emotional of what the desired result of a treatment should have been, or perhaps better said, what the result should not have been; these opinions all having some relationship with the concept of what the work originally looked like. It is outside the scope of this book to provide an exhaustive review of this literature. A number of important examples will, however, now be presented to serve as a basis for the further discussion on debates in conservation that follows in this chapter. S. Keck [1], for example, presented a brief history of controversies surrounding the so-called cleaning of works of art, where cleaning in art conservation generally means the removal of aged and discolored varnishes from paintings. There were works which had been considered by some experts to have been beautifully cleaned and restored, bringing back the beauty of the original colors to the paintings, whereas other experts considered them to have been badly damaged or ruined. Many of the emotional arguments against cleaning, which Keck discussed often, made use of terms such as "flayed" (e.g., National Gallery of London controversy, 1846–1853, and at the Louvre at about the same time), "ruined" (e.g., used by Pliny the Elder concerning the cleaning of a painting by Aristeidis; restoration of Leonardo's "Last Supper" in the 16th century; National Gallery of London cleaning controversy at the end of World War II), "scoured" or "scraped" (e.g., National Gallery of London controversy, 1846–1853), or "tasteless" (National Gallery of Art, Washington, D.C., 1978) to describe the final result of a treatment. A brief review of several literature sources of treatments which would be, if not frowned upon, totally forbidden today, carries the title "Scrubbers and Strippers?" [2].

Equally controversial is the question of what to do with past changes to a work of art ranging from old restoration treatments and retouches, to culturally or politically motivated overpainting, and even natural aging. There are those who argue that all changes to a work of art are part of the history of that work and should be retained. In the first modern theory of restoration for example, Cesare Brandi argues that past changes to a work of art are part of the history of the work and should therefore not be removed [3]. This includes discolored and darkened varnishes (as opposed to glazes intentionally used by the artist), an opinion which is still held by a number of conservators and questioned by others who favor the aesthetics of, for example, Leonardo da Vinci's "Mona Lisa" in something closer to its original form [4], whatever that may have been. Others argue that a work of art was created by its maker with some meaning or message that would be lost by all of the changes that were made later and cover up the original (see, e.g., one of the panel discussions in ref. [5]). In a nod to those who would want to retain the entire history of the object, they suggest that anything that is removed from a work should be properly documented and, if possible, physically saved for future generations to decide if they should be put back.

There are then the discussions about what to do with damaged or missing areas, so-called lacunae, in a work of art. For small damaged or missing areas, retouching the area to bring it back to its original appearance is considered permissible. However, most conservators will say that if a lacuna is too large, one should not attempt to "artistically" fill it to make the work complete, that is, one should not try to "guess" at what is missing in the original. There are a number of techniques which have been developed to fill lacunae, for example, in canvas and wall paintings, without distracting from the original parts of the work which are still visible, such as filling the lacunae with a neutral color or using various combinations of thin-striped patterns [6], for example, tratteggio [7], simulative retouching [8], and (a)chromatic techniques [9]. All of these techniques involve choices of color which make the infill blend in well with the rest of the work when viewed at a distance, but be obvious when observed very close to the work.

While the discussion up until now has dealt with paintings, it should not be forgotten that conservators are confronted with similar problems with the restoration of other forms of visual art. The question of whether to keep a change also comes up when it comes to additions to statues, decorative metal objects, and wall paintings in historic buildings. One sees the use of neutral-colored materials to reassemble sherds of ancient pottery back into their original form [e.g., 10], and the use of chromatic reintegration for retouching, for example, photographs [see e.g., 11, 12]. The filling of lacunae is also an issue for polychrome objects (see, e.g., 13, 14]), and questions always arise as to what kinds of materials a conservator is allowed to use to restore archeological and historic textiles [see e.g., 15, 16]. Finally, the choice of which layer of history to keep of a registered historic building and which to document and review is a frequent issue which needs consideration, for example, in older historic European buildings.

In the past several decades, an awareness has thus grown that decisions for treating an object are complex, and that there is no clear-cut, right or wrong solution for the treatment of a particular work of art; see, for example, the writings of G. Hedley on finding a proper balance of a painting when cleaning it [17]. When someone brings a work of art of value to a conservator, it is expected that the conservator not only has the practical capabilities for conducting eventual treatments but should also have sufficient theoretical expertise in all relevant aspects of art and art history for deciding what the desired results could be for each specific work that they are asked to consider and for deciding which result should be attained and how. In simplified form, the question becomes that of making better informed decisions as to what a conservator is allowed to do and what not.

1.2 Conservation codes of ethics

Dealing with what may and may not be done when conserving works of art and cultural heritage is the purview of so-called conservation ethics, or better said and as briefly alluded to in the previous section, Western-based conservation ethics. The question of what one is allowed to do and what not comes up in many critical professions such as genetic research, law, and medicine. Codes of ethics have been developed to help members of those professions in making often life-changing decisions and properly conducting their work.

The conservation profession is no different, and it is not a coincidence that the conservation and restoration of works of art and cultural heritage have often been compared to the treatment of human patients by medical professionals.

Examples of well-known Western conservation codes of ethics include those from the American Institute of Conservation (AIC) [18], the Australian Institute for Conservation of Cultural Material (AICCM) [19], the Canadian Association for Conservation of Cultural Property (CACCP) and the Canadian Association of Professional Conservators (CAPC) [20 or 21], the European Confederation of Conservator-Restorers' Organisations (ECCO) [22], and the Institute of Conservation (ICON) [23].

These codes of ethics lay out the framework of what a conservator is, what their qualifications should be, how they should professionally conduct themselves, and how they should deal with an object which is under their care. Current conservation codes of ethics are not just the result of the heated discussions mentioned in the previous section. They have, as their basis, thoughts and philosophies on conservation developed over the last two to three centuries.

Important thoughts on conservation in the past two centuries can be found in a Getty Institute review of issues in conservation [24]. The whole concept of preserving cultural heritage for the enjoyment and education of future generations is interwoven in most of the cited texts, but is exemplified by a quote from John Rushkin concerning architecture:

> Therefore, when we build, let us think that we build forever. Let it not be for present delight, not for present use alone; let it be such work as our descendants will thank us for, . . . and that men will say as they look upon the labor and wrought substance of them, 'See! this our fathers did for us.
>
> [25]

The first modern theory of restoration was developed and published in 1963 by Cesare Brandi, director of Istituto Centrale per il Restauro [26]. Brandi considered a number of aspects a conservator should think about when restoring a work of art or cultural heritage. In particular, related to the debate on cleaning, he was a strong proponent for preserving not only an original work of art or cultural heritage but also all of the changes that it has undergone. Besides leaving discolored varnishes, this also includes physical changes made by others to the work through the years, including overpainting and old restorations, even those of poor quality. He also warned conservators of the danger of the removal of glazes and tinted varnishes which the artist intentionally used [27]. In any case, this philosophy of retaining the history of an object was followed by many in the conservation field for years, and continues to be the subject of debate as to which "layer" of history should be preserved in an object and which can or should be removed. Opinions about the question of the removal of aged varnishes, which cover up the original appearance of the painting, as opposed to leaving it as an aesthetically or historically necessary patina [28] are made more complex given that many paintings by well-known artists have been varnished against the expressed wishes of the artist [29]. This then becomes a question of the artist's intent, which Albano warns is too often being put aside in conservation decisions [30].

The development of current conservation codes of ethics arguably has its roots in the cleaning controversy at the National Gallery of London after World War II. Many paintings which had been kept in hiding during the war were cleaned based on the results of scientific analysis. The idea was to bring the paintings back to their full glory and original color. The results polarized the art and art conservation world. On the one hand, the museum, of course, found the results to be beautiful and scientifically responsible, while on the other hand, those proponents of Brandi's theory found that the paintings had been ruined, and others questioned the aesthetics of bringing back original colors [31]. However, the cleaning controversy was not the only motivation for the development of conservation codes of ethics. Questions began to be raised about, for example, past restoration treatments such as wax-lining which irreversibly damaged paintings [32], what to do with overpainting on paintings and polychrome works in disagreement with Brandi's opinion that they should be left alone, whether one may replace original parts of an object with modern materials, and the issue of filling lacunae mentioned earlier.

The debate on these issues, and the debate on who is qualified to make decisions about these questions resulted in the strict codes of ethics which are in use today. In these codes, one sees a number of terms and concepts which broadly cover many of the controversial issues from the past, including, in alphabetical order,

i.   *aesthetics*, for example, "The conservator-restorer shall not remove material from cultural heritage unless this is indispensable for its preservation or it substantially interferes with the historic and aesthetic value of the cultural heritage" [22], or "The conservation professional should only recommend or undertake treatment that is judged suitable to the preservation of the aesthetic, conceptual, and physical characteristics of the cultural property" [18]

ii. *authenticity*, for example, "Declarations of age, origin, or authenticity should be made only when based on sound evidence" [18, 19]

iii. *appropriateness of a treatment*, for example, "You must have the appropriate conservation expertise and cultural, historical and technological knowledge to carry out the conservation measures you undertake" [23], or "The AICCM Member should only recommend or undertake treatment that is judged suitable to the preservation of the aesthetic, conceptual and physical characteristics of the cultural property, after thorough examination of all the evidence. When non-intervention best serves to

promote the preservation of the cultural property, it is appropriate to recommend that no treatment be performed" [19]

iv. *original*, for example, "Reconstruction is aimed at promoting an understanding of a cultural property, and is based on little or no original material but clear evidence of a former state" [CACCP/CAPC], or "Such
compensation [*for loss*] should be reversible and should not falsely
modify the known aesthetic, conceptual, and physical characteristics
of the cultural property, especially by removing or obscuring original
material" [18]

v. *respect (informed)* and *integrity*, for example, "all actions of the conservation professional must be governed by an informed respect for the
integrity of the property, including physical, conceptual, historical and
aesthetic considerations" [20, 21], or "The conservator-restorer shall
respect the aesthetic, historic and spiritual significance and the physical
integrity of the cultural heritage entrusted to her/his care" [22]

vi. *scientific investigation*, for example, "Materials and Methods: The conservation professional is responsible for choosing materials and methods
appropriate to the objectives of each specific treatment and consistent with currently accepted practice. The advantages of the materials
and methods chosen must be balanced against their potential adverse
effects on future examination, scientific investigation, treatment, and
function" [18], or "The AICCM Member should follow accepted scientific standards and research protocols. The AICCM Member should
use, issue or publish only such treatment proposals, reports or statements
that are thorough, accurate records of soundly based observation and/or
experiment and logical deductions there from. Testing on unique or rare
original materials/objects should be avoided where possible. Methods or
materials should not be used on original materials where there is no body
of evidence in existence to justify their use" [19].

vii. *significance*, for example, "It is recognised that the significance of cultural material may have a bearing on conservation decisions" [19], or
"All actions of the conservation professional must be governed by an
informed respect for the cultural property, its unique character and significance, and the people or person who created it" [18]

viii. *standards (highest possible)*, for example, "The conservation professional shall strive to attain the highest possible standards in all aspects of
conservation, including preventive conservation*, examination*, documentation*, research, treatment* and education."/"* All terms marked
with an asterisk are defined in the Glossary" [20, 21; also 19 but without
the asterisks]

Looking at these terms, one notes, as did Jonathan Ashley-Smith [33], that
they are written in fairly general principles and are, in fact, not particularly
well-defined. However, two things are fairly clear. One of the important

lessons to come out of the debates of the past and built into conservation codes of ethics is the requirement that conservators make sure that they have done all of the necessary art historical, historical and scientific research before making their treatment decisions. This is made clear in the terms iii, v, vi, and viii listed above. Along with this so-called informed respect for the object in their care, they must also understand what their treatments are doing with the materials with which an object was made. It was noted a number of times by participants of an invitation-only meeting of paintings conservators in 2001 that only "informed" conservators can do a good job [34].

The other clear message is that all of these guidelines are written using some form of the phrase "a conservator must/should/shall." The consequences of not following these guidelines can be found in no uncertain terms in some form or other, such as, "Violations of the Code and Guidelines that constitute unethical conduct may result in disciplinary action" [18, 19]. Again, as noted by Ashley-Smith [33], these consequences are reflected in the current strict interpretation of the codes, taught, in particular, in academic training programs for conservators, and still evident in much of the recent conservation and restoration literature.

Conservators have thus become fearful of the unknown and, as is popularly known, have obtained the reputation of nay-sayers. They want to leave no stone unturned before they dare to treat an object, actively or passively. The requirement that conservators have performed sufficient research combined with the threat of consequences if they do not follow the current strict interpretations of codes of ethics has led to a strong dependence on scientific research. It should therefore not come as a surprise that they have turned more and more to science and engineering for assistance, with the common underlying belief that science and engineering are "objective" and thus provide a solid basis for their decisions. This has led to the development and the significant role that conservation science and, more recently, the related field known as technical art history play in the conservation of works of art.

1.3   Brief history of science-based conservation

It is generally agreed that modern science-based conservation, as it is now known, also began in earnest with the previously discussed cleaning controversy at the National Gallery of London. At the time, it was argued that scientific and, more specifically, chemical analysis techniques were used to determine how to safely "clean" paintings stored during the war, and bring them back to their "original" colors and appearance; see again [31].

Since then, a veritable alphabet soup of scientific techniques has been developed and modernized with innovations involving ever higher precision and resolution, all the way down to atomic levels. Many of these techniques have been extremely valuable to conservators and art historians for determining the chemical composition and condition of art materials and for understanding their aging processes. The results of these scientific analyses, along with art historical research, provide conservators the information they need to make the better-informed decisions they are required by conservation ethics to make. However, one can question what the use is of many of the latest innovations down to "nano" and "atomic" levels.

A comprehensive and chronological history of developments in conservation science and science-based conservation may be interesting at this point, but is beyond the scope of this book. Instead, a number of historically important developments in conservation science will be briefly introduced in this section. Several examples of recent innovations will also be introduced. The purpose is to give the reader a feel for what has been happening in recent years technologically in art conservation in preparation for the further discussion in this book. In that sense, it is more useful to describe the selected technologies within the framework of the general procedure for scientifically studying works of art before conservation decisions are made.

The procedure is actually quite similar to engineering failure analysis, which the author also performed before entering the cultural heritage field. A work of art which requires restoration has, in a certain sense, "failed" in its function in the same way some commercial product has failed. In order to find solutions, that is, the reason for the failure and improvements in product design, or restoration treatments for the work of art, it is important to obtain as much information as possible about an object in its current state, before eventually having to alter or destroy macroscopic evidence in order to obtain more detailed microscopic evidence.

When conservation scientists are asked to investigate the condition of a particular work of art, or engineers to conduct failure analysis, the first techniques they therefore turn to are nondestructive in nature, where nondestructive means exactly what it says. The work of art is not physically disturbed; no samples are taken. The most obvious but often underrated instrument to be used for this work is, of course, the naked eye. The initial investigation of the work is, or in any case should be, performed with, among others, the conservator and (art) historian. The goal is to obtain visual information in order to better identify and describe the conservation issue at hand and to be able to place it within the context of the work. As the team looks in more detail, they will eventually need to make use of some form of magnifying lens and stereomicroscopes, and if the object is small enough, light microscopes. A camera, earlier analogue but now mostly digital, is also indispensable. Visible light is in all cases the main source of illumination.

It is noted that, at this early stage of the initial failure analysis, one can already question how objectively the conservation scientist and the conservation team are working. As can be seen in Section 1.2, the entire historical philosophy and debate on conservation is rife with, what more and more cultural heritage professionals are willing to admit, what are known as "subjective" opinions. In modern daily science-based conservation, and this is no different from engineering failure analysis, an added problem is that the investigating team, more often than not, already begins to speculate on possible treatments and/or the final result without having collected all the necessary technical information. Taking this a step further, it is also debatable as to whether science really is objective as it is made out to be. Even though a scientific instrument may be computerized or expensive and able to produce data in a high-tech form, the data are, more often than not, subject to interpretation, especially in conservation science where it is difficult to obtain "sufficient" data to make a decision on something that is unique, valuable, and old. And the scientific instrument itself was designed for some purpose of which one could also question its "objectivity." Be that as it may, this question of what objectivity, or for that matter, what subjectivity is, is beyond the scope of this book. What will be a recurring theme in this book on innovative technologies is, however, what role this perceived dichotomy of objectivity and subjectivity plays in conservation science and conservation decision-making.

During the first half of the 20th century, before the advent of what is now being called modern science-based conservation, it was found that ultraviolet (UV) light and x-rays, both of which are not visible to the naked eye, were also quite useful in art conservation [35]. The use of UV light has since become a standard method for detecting, among others, old varnishes or remnants thereof, glues, and other resins. The technique makes use of the property of many such materials, that they give off visible light, fluoresce, only while being irradiated with UV light.

The use of x-rays in the study of works of art also developed during this time. X-rays, as is well-known from medicine, can penetrate an object and reveal, for example, the supporting structure for bronze statues (see, e.g., [36, 37]), or retouches or changes in paintings (see, e.g., [38]). This is possible because different materials allow more or less radiation to pass through them. One can thus see the iron-supporting structure in a bronze statue for the same reason that one can see the skeleton in a human body. Since the development of x-ray computer tomography techniques in medicine and industry, three-dimensional x-ray images of objects are now possible.

Until roughly several decades ago, these techniques were pretty much the limit of what conservation scientists could do in terms of nondestructive analysis. In the second half of the 20th century, a number of technical innovations took place, which would have major significance for modern-day analysis of works of art. One was the development by Van Asperen de Boer of infrared reflectography (IRR) to reveal underdrawings in paintings (see, among others, [39, 40]). IRR makes use of the fact that most paints are transparent to infrared light, but carbon, which is used in various forms such as charcoal, is not. One can thus see "under" the paint layer and find the original sketches which an artist made using charcoal before producing the final work. Since then, the technique has been optimized in many ways, including the use of digital imaging systems which can image entire works. Such systems not only improve the spatial resolution of the images but also allow for fine-tuning the infrared wavelengths used in order to assist in nondestructively identifying certain pigments which do absorb certain wavelengths of infrared radiation (see, e.g., [41, 42]).

Another technical innovation important for nondestructive testing was the use of x-rays for what is known as x-ray fluorescence (XRF) spectroscopy. XRF has become a standard nondestructive technique for determining the elemental composition of materials in all kinds of works of art. Simply put, an x-ray beam is focused on the work, and it knocks electrons out of certain shells of the atoms at that location. Electrons from higher shells fall into the now empty shell, and an x-ray is released – characteristic of the energy difference between the two shells. Since all elements of the periodic system have a unique[2] set of electrons and corresponding energies, one can determine which elements are in, for example, a particular paint on a work of art. Examples of XRF spectra are shown in Fig. 1.1, where one sees graphs with the number of electrons (counts) on the vertical axis at a particular energy on the horizontal axis. Based on the relationships between the peaks and with the assistance of reference measurements made on known materials, an experienced user can obtain a good idea, for example, of which pigments were used in a particular work of art. Though XRF has been commercially available since the 1950s using table- or floor-mounted instruments [43, 44], the development of handheld XRF instruments with sufficient resolutions was one of the major innovations which led to their now common and important use in the conservation field for analyzing objects which cannot be transported to the laboratory, objects such as very valuable paintings, wall paintings, or large polychrome statues.

X-rays can also be used to help identify crystalline materials using the concept of Bragg diffraction [44]. Most metals, ceramics, and mineral-based pigments have a repeating crystal structure analogous to the stacking of tennis or ping-pong balls, where atoms are bonded at specific angles and distances. X-ray diffraction (XRD) techniques make use of an x-ray beam of a particular wavelength. A narrow beam focused on the specimen will be reflected only at particular angles, depending on the positions of the atoms in the crystal structure and the distance between them. Based on these angles, one can calculate the distance between the atoms and their spatial relationship to each other, that is, the crystal structure. The material can be identified by comparing the data to measurements made on reference materials. XRD is used, for example, to determine the crystal structure of historical metal objects, and thus how they were processed, or help identify different chemically similar or identical forms of mineral pigments such as rutile and anatase titanium white or iron oxides [46, 47]. For the precision and resolution required of this technique, XRD is not portable, and, in fact, in many cases cannot be considered nondestructive since the samples for a standard x-ray diffractometer must be small or have a certain geometry. Powder diffraction techniques are, however, nondestructive when used to analyze, for example, samples of historical pigment powders.

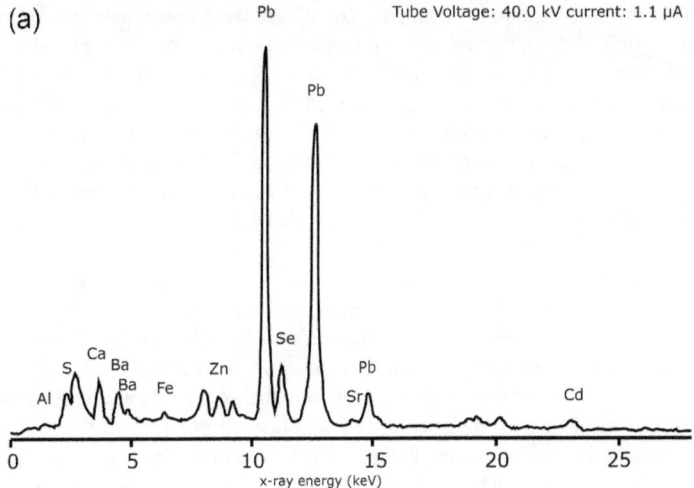

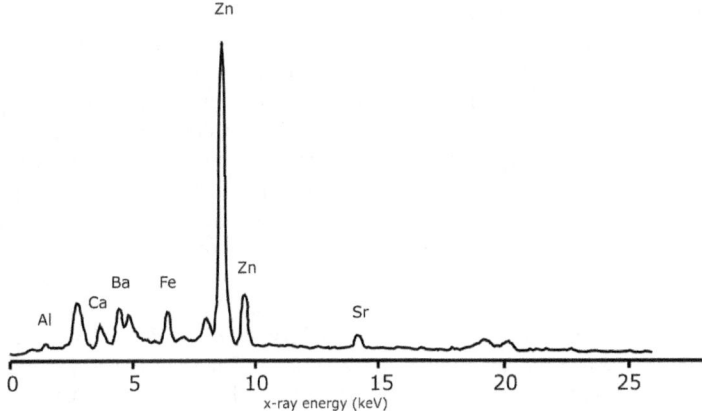

Fig. 1.1 Examples of XRF spectra for (figures adapted and used by permission from [45])
a) white ground layer from Lucio Fontana, "Concetto spaziale. Notte d'amore a Venezia" (1960).
b) yellow paint layer from Karel Appel, "La grande fleur de la nuit" (1954).

XRF does have the limitation that, with only a few exceptions, it can only be used to identify elemental composition. Knowing which elements are in a material is, however, not at all sufficient for determining the chemical state of the material in, among others, its current aged condition. Electron energies are slightly different when they are bonded to other elements in molecules, and XRF does not have the resolution to measure these slight differences. In particular, XRF cannot say anything about the chemical state of organic, non-crystalline, and/or synthetic materials such as many natural varnishes and paint binders, consolidants, adhesives, plastics, and other synthetic materials. Many such materials consist of molecules containing complex bonds of carbon, hydrogen, and oxygen. XRF can only detect the presence of carbon and oxygen, but not how they are bonded.

In order to determine bonding states and thus get to the specific and detailed identification of artist materials, the conservation scientist has to resort to destructive techniques for materials analysis. With a few (handheld) exceptions described below, these techniques are destructive, at the least in the sense that one needs to take a sample from the work of art, and at the most, because one actually has to destroy the sample while analyzing it.

As an aside, a first of a number of critical looks in this book is taken at the concept of "innovative technology in art conservation." Many of the research groups that have continued the further optimization of the techniques, which are about to be discussed, are wont to call their work innovative, with the implication that a contributing factor to their innovativeness is that they are "nondestructive." However, if one reads more closely, the techniques are non-destructive, but only for the specimen. The fact of the matter is, one must take a specimen from the work of art, which is destructive and something that conservators and art historians would like to minimize as much as possible.

Be that as it may, techniques which do not destroy the sample are those which use some form of radiation for analysis including forms of light not visible to the human eye (ultraviolet and infrared), visible light, electrons, and x-rays in techniques besides XRF. In order to determine the specific chemical state of a material used in a work of art, conservation scientists resort to a number of analysis techniques using these types of radiation, but which also require ever smaller samples. The samples can then be measured to ever finer details, technically speaking, and can be measured at ever higher resolution. A number of techniques use beams of UV, visible, and/or infrared light focused on the material samples. A specific kind of molecular bond will alter the incoming beam at particular wavelengths of the incoming light source. One therefore obtains a graph of the change in intensity of light for each wavelength, with valleys at those specific wavelengths. The material can be identified using these graphs, so-called spectra, by comparing them with reference spectra measured on known materials.

A well-known technique for studying organic materials is Fourier-transform infrared (FTIR) spectroscopy. This technique uses infrared light with wavelengths between roughly 2.5 to 25 micrometers (μm) on a thin specimen. Most of the light passes through the specimen, but some of it is absorbed at energies (wavelengths) corresponding to the energies of the molecular bonds in the material. One obtains a spectrum in a graph of intensity, or specifically, transmittance (how much light gets through the material to the detector), on the vertical axis and wavelength on the horizontal axis. An example of such results is shown in Fig. 1.2. The drops in transmittance correspond to certain molecular bonding energies. By comparing such results to reference data, one can identify the material. In this example, one sees the chemical state of a fresh paint medium, compressed linseed oil, and that of the oil after drying and artificially aged for one. One sees that the peaks shift with aging time.

Conducting spectral measurements using ultraviolet and visible light (UV-VIS) works according to the same principle. It is noted that visible light spectroscopy characterizes material by their "color"[3] ("reflectance spectra"). This will be discussed in more detail in Chapter 3.

The use of light is useful for examining entire objects or samples thereof. However, it has its limits in terms of spatial resolution. In the case of the techniques described previously, this limit can be the wavelength of light, roughly 0.4 μm for blue light sources, and/or the diameter of the beam used to probe the specimen. Many conservation issues require, however, studying the properties of materials and surfaces at sub-micrometer levels. Again, a number of techniques have been adopted from science and engineering, which have proved invaluable to art conservation. The most valuable is scanning electron microscopy (SEM), nowadays almost always combined with energy dispersive spectroscopy (EDS), also known as energy dispersive x-ray analysis (EDX or EDAX). Instead of light, SEM makes use of a high-powered beam of electrons in order to image a surface. A basic SEM does this in two ways.

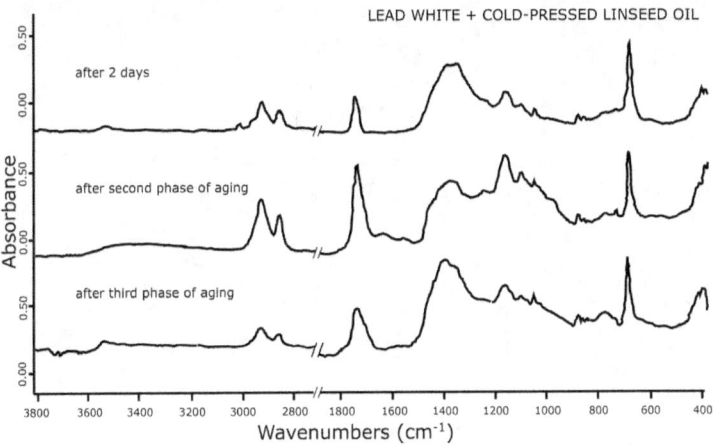

Fig. 1.2 FTIR spectroscopy showing from top to bottom, changes due to aging of lead white + cold-pressed linseed oil paint [used by permission of the author of 48]

If an electron beam strikes a surface, it either knocks electrons out of the surface into the detector (secondary electrons), or the beam is reflected into a detector (back-scattering). The secondary electron mode is commonly used to image the surface topography, looking at, for example, changes in surfaces due to conservation treatments, micro-cracking, fracture surfaces, and corrosion products. An example of a fracture surface from an outdoor sculpture is shown in Fig. 1.3. In the backscattering mode, the image depends on the atomic mass of the elements in the material and their distribution. Depending on how strongly the electron beam is reflected, one can get a rough indication of the distribution of elements.

The SEM is commonly used in combination with EDS (SEM-EDS) to identify pigments in cross-sections of paint samples. EDS is essentially the same technique as XRF except that the radiation source is the electron beam instead of an x-ray beam. The main advantage of EDS over XRF is that the electron beam size is on the order of 30 nm, much smaller than one can obtain with an x-ray beam. Using backscatter imaging, one can locate particles which one wants to analyze, and then aim the electron beam directly on them to do the elemental analysis. Since the microscope is "scanning," one can also

(a)

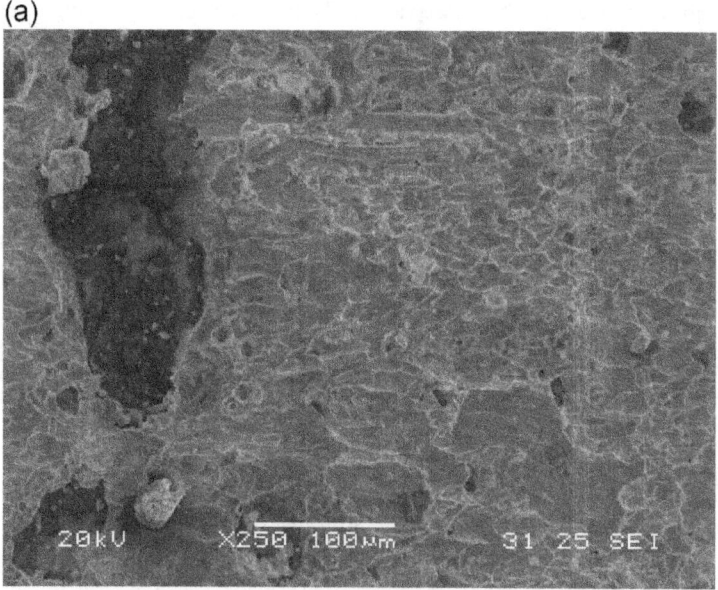

Fig. 1.3 Scanning electron microscope (SEM) images

a – secondary SEM image of the failure of a joint between copper windings and steel skeleton from "Tong van Lucifer," later renamed "Tong" (Lucifer Tongue/Tongue) (1993) by Ruud van de Wint

b – loose copper windings on "Tong van Lucifer"

(b)

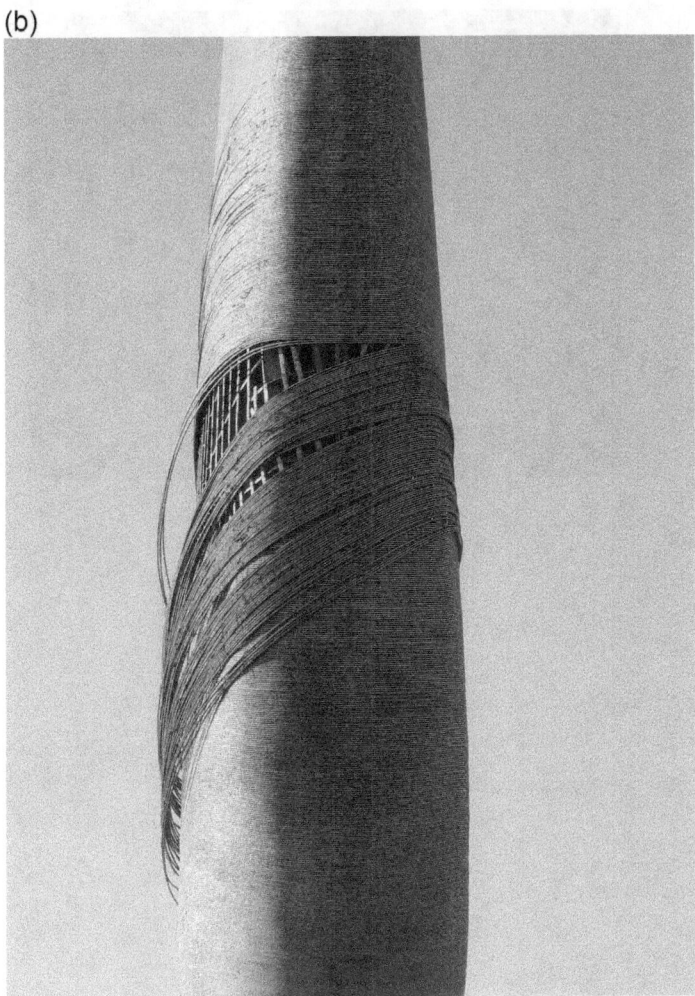

Fig. 1.3 (Continued)

conduct an EDS analysis on a whole surface looking for a particular element. An example of the identification of pigments from a project led by the author in a painting using SEM-EDS is shown in Fig. 1.4.

A major disadvantage of the SEM is that the analysis must be conducted on small specimens which fit in a vacuum chamber of roughly 10^{-5} Pascals (10^{-10} standard atmospheric pressure) so that the electron beam is not disturbed and dispersed by air molecules. Such a vacuum level is, however, not suitable for

(a)

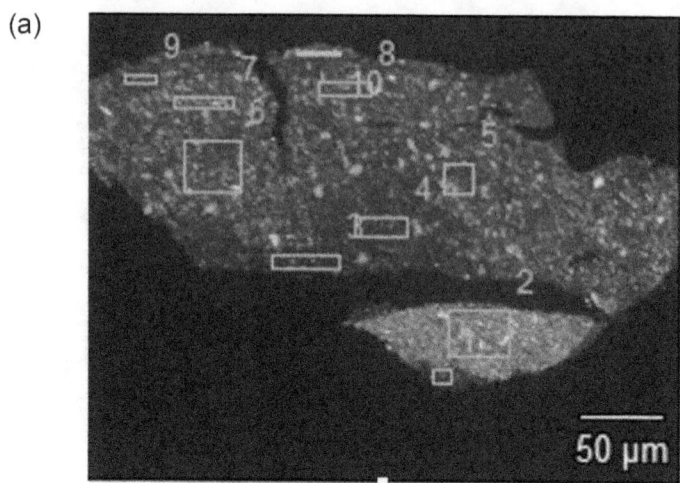

(b)

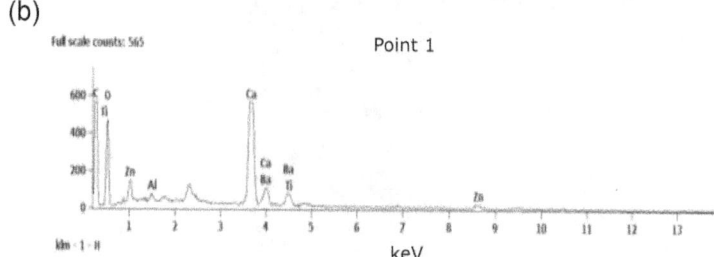

(c)

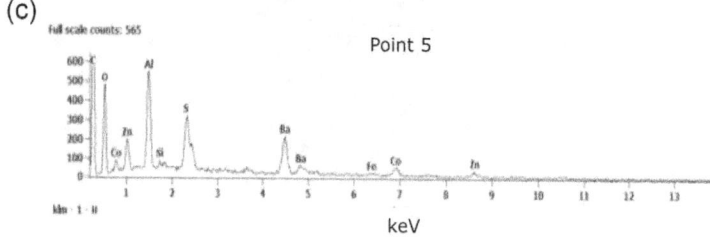

Fig. 1.4 SEM-EDS of paints in a cross-section taken from "Blauwe Tafel" (Blue Table, 1977) by Jan Roeland [49].

a) Backscatter image of a paint sample showing analysis locations

b) EDS spectrum for location 2 (possible ground layer with barium sulphate and possibly zinc, lead, and titanium white)

c) EDS spectrum for location 5 (paint layer with barium sulphate, cobalt blue, ochre, and possibly zinc and titanium white) studying many organic solids and plastics which may tend to outgas, ruining both the specimen and the SEM chamber. Furthermore, the electron beam is a current, just like the electrons which go through wires as electric current. If the electron beam is used to study a nonconducting material, it will build up a charge on the specimen surface, which will cause it to "glow" so that nothing can be seen, and/or will literally burn (oxidize) the specimen. This problem can be solved by lightly coating nonconductive specimens with a conducting film of carbon or gold. However, in the past 20 years, the development of so-called low-vacuum SEMs has allowed scientists to study many nonconducting specimens without such measures. There are also SEM models available with large chambers in which small objects can fit.

Finally, there are still many types of samples, in particular, of organic materials which require further destructive analysis. Destructive analyses must, of course, be conducted last, as the specimen will then no longer be accessible. One of the most commonly known destructive analysis techniques is the examination of cross-sections of materials such as paint samples. For such an analysis, the specimen is embedded in a transparent resin such as epoxy. The section is then highly polished and viewed in a light microscope. Obviously, the specimen can no longer be recovered. There are various types of lighting which can be used to accentuate particular features of the specimen, including UV, polarized light, dark and light field, and other filters. The technology has advanced from identifying pigments just by color and appearance, to being able to determine chemical composition in the SEM-EDS, calculating the percentages of pigments in paint mixtures, and mapping their distribution.

For the analysis of organic materials such as paint binders, destructive chemical techniques are used, which involve separating the material into various components and identifying those components. The material can be identified by comparing the results with reference data taken on known samples of pure materials. Two techniques which are often used include high-performance liquid chromatography (HPLC) and gas chromatography–mass spectrometry (GC-MS) [50]. In HPLC, the sample is dissolved and its components separated. The different components are detected using various kinds of detectors, often making use of the absorption of various wavelengths of light, hence the word chromatography. In GC-MS, the sample is heated and evaporated, and separates into a number of components. A mass spectrometer detects their mass, and the spectrum of masses is compared to reference data in order to identify the material.

The analysis techniques, which have just been described, can be found in most well-equipped conservation laboratories. However, even those techniques have their limits, and for many difficult conservation problems, efforts have focused in the past two decades in refining many techniques in order to be able to measure ever smaller "micro" or "nano" quantities of complex artist materials. Beginning with mass spectrometry, there are a number of other techniques, which have been developed in recent years, to help identify specific types of materials or to study small samples (see, e.g., the review in [51]). A recent innovation is the use of lasers for separating components of a material. For example, in matrix-assisted laser desorption ionization-time-of-flight mass spectrometry (MALDI-TOF MS), the sample is ionized using a laser and the components are accelerated through an electric field. The time it takes for the components to arrive at the detector (time-of-flight, TOF) depends on their molecular weight. MALDI-TOF MS is useful for the analysis of very small samples on the order of micro-grams. A further innovation is the use of a laser to essentially burn a small point on the surface of a specimen, laser-induced breakdown spectroscopy (LIBS). The heat of the laser creates a micro-plasma above the specimen. As it cools, the plasma emits light at certain wavelengths which are detected creating a spectrum, which can be compared with reference data. In art conservation, LIBS was developed in combination with the still controversial use of lasers for the cleaning of works of art.

A technique which has recently become quite valuable in conservation science is Raman spectroscopy. This technique makes use of weak signals resulting from the interaction of monochromatic (single wavelength) radiation with molecular bonds known as the Raman effect. It is useful as a complementary technique to FTIR, described earlier. FTIR is useful for determining bonds between different elements (carbon, hydrogen, and oxygen), while Raman is effective for measuring bonds between the same element such as various types of carbon-carbon bonds. The use of lasers and the development of high-resolution digital sensors now allow scientists to detect Raman signals and identify even the smallest individual pigments on the order of 1 μm in size, but also mixtures of very similar pigments [52]. Both FTIR and Raman are now standard instruments in many conservation science laboratories. Recently, they have become available in portable versions, allowing them to be brought to the object.

A more recent and exotic technique, which has received considerable publicity from the museums and research institutes that have access to it, is the use of synchrotron radiation at the few national or international particle accelerators found around the world, such as CERN (Geneva), CHESS (Cornell University, USA), or AGLAE (C2RMF/Louvre) and Soleil (Paris). These accelerators were originally developed for research in particle physics and the development of new energy sources. The various types of radiation such accelerators produce are much more powerful than those provided by commercial laboratory instruments, and often with much better spatial resolution. The accelerators have seen increasing use in many fields of physics, biology, medicine, and engineering (see, e.g., [53]) and have occasionally seen use for the study of works of art and archeology (see, e.g., [54]). Examples include elemental analysis similar to XRF but then with particles as the excitation radiation, so-called PIXE (particle-induced x-ray emission) and so-called Rutherford backscattering spectroscopy (RBS), which measures the energy of reflected particles as a function of the mass of the elements which the particles are striking [55]. For XRD, the use of high-powered synchrotron beams at international accelerators has become popular among institutions which can afford it and can get an appointment for the limited time slots that are available. X-radiation at such facilities provides smaller beam sizes but with more power to allow the micro-analysis (μXRD) of, for example, archeological materials with complex mixtures of crystalline materials, and even determine the amount of amorphous material present (see, e.g., [54, 56, 57]). Although beam time itself is, in general, free, it is difficult to come by, and the experiments are labor-intensive in the sense that they involve round-the-clock measurements and analysis by a rotating team of experts.

What has been presented in the previous paragraphs has essentially been the chemical aspects of conservation science, the analysis of the materials of a work of art in order to determine its current state and to give an indication of its original state. It is, of course, the many chemical changes which change the appearance of an object as it ages, and it is a chemical conservation treatment which will change the appearance of the aged object into something that someone will define as acceptable or not.

This question of appearance brings up one of the most important technological developments in art conservation, that of digital imaging and color science. On the one hand, these technologies provide museums and art conservators with the capability of accurately documenting works of art at high color and spatial resolution. On the other hand, new nondestructive tools for chemical analyses have been made possible by matching color spectra with the results of chemical analyses. It is now possible to identify many pigments by their "color" as mentioned previously (VIS spectroscopy), map particular pigments and their materials across a work of art, and predict their original appearance.

Up to now, the discussion of conservation science has focused on the analysis of the materials in an object. In the last two to three decades, conservation science has also made significant contributions to the field of preventive conservation, in particular, in the areas of museum climate and lighting control. The development of specialized HVAC (heating, ventilation, and air conditioning) systems for museums and showcases came in response to increasing calls for strict limits on temperature and relative humidity toward the end of the 20th century. Also important in terms of environment have been developments in monitoring and controlling indoor air pollution in terms of gases which are chemically reactive, in particular sulfides and acids from outdoor air brought into the museum and/or outgassing from showcase and building materials as well as the objects themselves (see, e.g., [58, 59]).

Another important development in the last several decades is the realization that the fading and discoloration of objects due to ultraviolet and visible light depends not only on the intensity of the light source but also how long the object is exposed to the light. In technical terms, object fading depends on how much light in units of lux the object is exposed to, but also how much time. The total exposure is then given in terms of lux-hours. Guidelines have been developed for different classes of objects, with photographs, paper, and books being the most sensitive. Recently developed micro-faders are seeing increasing use for unobtrusively testing light stability directly on real objects. Museums can now make informed decisions as to how often they can exhibit light-sensitive objects, and what light levels they use so that (older) visitors can still see and appreciate any colors and contrasts in the objects being displayed.

While these scientific developments in preventive concentration have significantly improved the ability to slow degradation processes in works of art, there are still subjective issues which need to be decided when implementing preventive technologies. Degradation processes most often involve changes to the color and appearance of an object, and how much change is acceptable within a given period. The issue of color and appearance will be discussed further in Chapter 3 of this book. Another issue of intense subjective debate is whether museum climate limits need to be so strict (see, e.g., [60]).

1.4   Innovative technology in art conservation

In the previous section, the development of conservation science in the last century and, in particular, since the National Gallery cleaning controversy was briefly reviewed. The purpose was not to provide a comprehensive review of the field but to show how conservation science developed to fill the recognized need for conservators to properly inform themselves before making difficult decisions on the treatment of works of art. It has also made important contributions to understanding how works of art age, and perhaps coming closer to the elusive goal of determining how a work originally appeared.

It can thus certainly be argued, and many members of the conservation profession would wholeheartedly agree, that innovation in conservation science has resulted in the development and optimization of a wide range of innovative and complementary nondestructive and destructive analysis techniques, techniques which have certainly brought conservation a long way since the middle of the 20th century. There have been a number of important innovations along the way, starting with the use of infrared light to study underdrawings, various complementary techniques for chemical analysis including the development of techniques to deal with samples much smaller than chemists in many commercial laboratories will ever have to deal with, and high-resolution digital imaging for nondestructive analysis as well as producing true color images. Advances in preventive conservation have also increased the "lifetime" of objects and, in many cases, reduced the need to restore them as often.

The reader may have noted at some point during this discussion of conservation science that most innovations in conservation science involve measuring things in ever increasing detail and with ever increasing precision. This has, in fact, vastly improved how conservators approach objects, providing them with more information about the works of art in their care so that they can make proper decisions to actively (or not) conserve them. With the many available analysis techniques, conservators can now treat each work of art as an individual problem, as opposed to dealing with them in general classes of objects, as was done in the past. The ability to identify materials down to sub-micron levels has also help conservators in identifying and dealing with the many original and sometimes complex materials which artists made themselves, or identifying unknown varnishes which seem to resist any type of chemical cleaning treatment.

In combination with art historical and historical research, conservators and art historians and conservation scientists have thus been able to make great progress in understanding how works of art were made, the context in which they were made, how they age, and how they must be cared for, either with active treatment or with preventive conservation. This has led to the development of a new interdisciplinary field known as technical art history. This cooperation is also leading to innovative work to try to determine how works of art originally appeared and reproduce them for study and for the general public as well.

Having read all of these arguments, one could conclude that innovation in art conservation has been a great success and is absolutely necessary in the future to preserve cultural heritage for future generations. But is that so? A case in point is the aforementioned work in preventive conservation on climate control. HVAC systems designed for the strict climate conditions of the end of the 20th century have been found to be expensive and, for small museums, unaffordable. Environmental awareness and the volatility of energy supplies and prices have raised the question as to whether climate limits can be made more flexible. Museums and collection managers are now questioning the strict climate conditions, supported by new developments in methods for collection risk assessment combined with determinations of the significance and value of individual and collections of works of art (see, e.g., [61–64]). However, these risk analysis methodologies have a glaring weakness. They rely on assumptions about the effect of climate changes on materials of works of arts, but the fact of the matter is, there is still little knowledge and understanding of how climate affects the lifetime of materials. This author has heard many conservators and conservation scientists claim that the problem is too complex and that it is not possible to accurately model the effect of climate on object degradation. The author finds this to be a lame excuse not to attack the problem, again combined with the fear of the unknown and conservation codes of ethics. It is reminded that Robert Feller actually conducted work on chemical reaction kinetics (how fast reactions proceed) [65], but little work has been done to follow that up.

Other examples of innovations which have questionable use are that developed to protect works of art from vibrations in transport or due to activities such as construction or rock concerts in or near museums. Museums go to great lengths to protect objects from the effects of vibrations due to art transport or due to activities in or near the museums, although there is very little understanding of what vibrations are and how they affect the condition of objects in the heritage world, and virtually no data are available, except for the limited data this author has produced. Yet, one often sees overly expensive innovations in protective measures against vibrations, which are not based on any "failure" criteria for the objects they are supposedly protecting. Furthermore, so-called innovative vibration monitors monitor shock and not vibrations.

And then there is the question as to how much detail one really needs to know in order to make a "proper" conservation decision. This author's experience is that far too many conservators want to conduct research on literally every possible parameter, which could possibly negatively impact an object. This is based on the fear of failure instilled by the strict interpretation of conservation codes of ethics. Unfortunately, too many conservation scientists play into this fear with a continuous stream of so-called innovations.

It is useful at this point to consider the definition of the word "innovation." The Cambridge online dictionary gives the following definitions [66] for innovation:

- (the use of) a new idea or method
- a new idea or method, or the use of new ideas and methods
- a new idea, design, product, etc.
- the development of new products, designs, or ideas.

However, in everyday usage, innovation has become strongly associated with the word "technology," and, with that, with words like "advanced," "good," "improved," and "modern." And far too many people blindly believe that something that is "innovative" must be good, until it is too late. Society has seen many improvements in the quality of life with the introduction of plastics, and it is only now recognizing the effect that they have on the environment, the protests of the manufacturers and their suppliers notwithstanding. And anything having to do with digital technologies is still considered to be innovative and necessary to "improve" our lives, even though it creates more stress by speeding up work processes and producing an overabundance of information, and this all in the age of fake news and political turmoil. The conservation world also misinterprets the word "innovation."

It is recalled that the requirement for being properly informed was a conclusion drawn from the debates surrounding the cleaning of paintings as well as other treatments from the 19th and early 20th centuries. The requirement then became one of the important pillars of conservation codes of ethics, codes which have, in the last decades, been very strictly interpreted. The strict interpretations continue to be the source of criticism and heated debate about many conservation decisions. Which conservator in their right mind would then want to take the risk of being accused of ruining an object because they did not check out that one last scientific detail?

But this raises the question as to what it means to "ruin" an object, a concept first introduced by Pliny the Elder, as noted in Section 1.1. While increasing numbers of conservators and art historians appear to have accepted that attaining the original appearance of a work of art is not possible, the enormous effort to precisely identify the materials and their chemical state in objects, find and reproduce original paint recipes, and, finally, produce realistic or true color reproductions seems to indicate that the opposite is true. Does "ruining" an object then imply making it impossible to ever again bring the object anywhere close to its original state or at least to a state which still expresses the original intentions of its maker? Or is it a question of not having reached a "proper" balance when cleaning an aged painting, as discussed by Hedley and others [17]?

Many scientists and engineers continue to prey on this combination of fear of ruining a work of art and a desire for original appearance with yet another innovation, selling it more often than not with some version of the phrase, "We hope that this research helps to determine how the object looked originally." Many museums, conservators, as well as research funding agencies then gobble up the latest in high-profile innovative scientific instrumentation and analysis techniques to measure the state of high-profile objects down to almost atomic levels in the belief that this will lead to even better understanding of works of art and how they originally appeared, and, not in the least, to score publicity.

The question of what constitutes original appearance is not only a matter of precision measurements and calculations. What is often forgotten, not only by scientists but also by art historians and conservators as well, is that decisions about how objects are supposed to look after treatment are quite subjective in nature. There is a large body of research on the perception of works of art, how their original appearance must be understood based on studies of artists' intent, the historical context in which they worked, and the ever-changing context and perception of viewers throughout history. Most conservators and funding officials do not have the technical background to understand what innovative technologies claim to be offering, and then question whether those innovations even help them in ultimately making their conservation decisions.

In the rest of this book, this concept of "objective" technological innovation being used to bring back some semblance of original or balanced appearance will therefore be critically examined, in other words, this tension between objectivity and subjectivity. Although any field of conservation science is open to critical examination including the work of this author, the focus of this book will be on the ultimate end products – the appearance of works of art as predicted and produced by so-called innovations in the fields of color science, digital imaging, and digital reproductions. Chapter 2 will first examine what it is that people actually see when they look at works of art, and how scientists in other fields are trying to understand human perception. It will be shown that people do not see works of art the way art historians, conservators, and other heritage professionals think or would like them to see them. Chapter 3 will then focus on the concept of color and the perception of color. It will be postulated that the use of the term color science for everything that has to do with the appearance and perception of color is misleading, given that color is a cultural construct and not something objective. The question again rises as to whether people actually perceive colors the way art historians and color scientists think they do.

Furthermore, color is also not the only characteristic of a work of art which a viewer sees and perceives. In Chapter 4, the role of surface texture/roughness on how objects appear will be discussed. Quantitative methods for measuring roughness and providing some quantitative measure for the concepts of gloss or matteness will again show the problems of dealing with subjective matter using objective measurements and arguments. Gloss, for example, can supposedly be measured objectively using techniques borrowed from the engineering world, but as with color, the interpretation of the results of such measurements can be lost in the subjective terms which are used to describe them. The combined use of color science and surface texture for producing high-resolution "true-color" reproductions of works of art and how they may have looked originally will be critically examined in Chapter 5. In particular, there is an analogy to be drawn between the effect that photography had on the field of art history, and the effect that the current innovative development digital color images will have on how works of art are viewed, a new reality in the appearance and perception of art. The dangers of such so-called innovations in terms of counterfeits and forgeries will also be examined.

In Chapter 6, it is cautioned that the field of art conservation needs to approach technological innovation with more informed thought and care. The limited understanding of how works of art age and, more importantly, the lack of "failure criteria" conservators use to determine when an object must be restored continues to lead to overly expensive solutions looking for a problem. In the case of color science and digital imaging technology, this has led to the creation of a "new reality" in the viewing and perception of works of art, created at great expense and sacrificing research funding for more research into solutions for more important but mundane issues in conservation.

1.5   Summary of Chapter 1

In this chapter, the background for the further discussion in this book of technological innovations in art conservation has been developed. The question of why works of art are conserved was briefly examined in terms of the search for originality and/or authenticity of a work in need of restoration. This was followed by a brief review of the heated debate throughout the centuries about what a good restoration is, that is, what one is allowed to do and how one could otherwise ruin a work of art. This debate culminated in the cleaning controversy at the National Gallery in London after World War II, which led in part to the development of codes of ethics for conservation, which are written in general terms but have become strictly interpreted in the past decades. This has resulted in a fear of failure, that is, ruining an object, among members of the conservation profession. A concomitant result of the cleaning controversy was the rapid development of the field of conservation science to fulfill a perceived need for a good objective scientific basis for conservation decisions, and also fueled by a fear of making a wrong, insufficiently informed conservation decision.

A number of important innovations and developments in scientific analysis techniques were described, which have proven quite valuable for understanding the materials which objects are made of, their properties, and aging, and has assisted conservators in making subjective decisions in many difficult situations. However, the term innovation is widely misused. Innovation means new, but has also become associated with the word good. It is argued that both the conservation field and the conservation science field must consider more carefully what is actually necessary in terms of technological innovations, given the uncertainty and vagaries of what and how professionals and the general public actually see and perceive in works of art. The rest of this book will critically examine these issues of the advantages and disadvantages of using objective innovative technologies in color science and digitalization in art conservation for supporting subjective conservation decisions based partly on fear of failure.

Notes

1 It is noted, however, that the profession of the conservation of art or cultural heritage in general is, in any case, not officially recognized anywhere in the world, as, for example, most medical professions are. Therefore, anyone can set up shop and call themselves a conservator/restorer.
2 With a few exceptions.
3 The reasons for the quotation marks will become apparent in Chapter 3.

References

1. Sheldon Keck, 'Some Picture Cleaning Controversies: Past and Present', *Journal of the American Institute for Conservation*, 23.2 (1984), 73–87.
2. Harriet Owen Hughes, 'Scrubbers and Strippers?', *The Picture Restorer*, 10 (1996), 13–15.
3. Cesare Brandi, Chapter 5 – 'Restoration with Regard to the Historical Case' and Chapter 6 – 'Restoration with Regard to the Aesthetic Case', in *Theory of Restoration*, English edn, Istituto Centrale per il Restauro (Firenze: Naridini Editore, 2005), pp. 65–75.

4. *Personal Viewpoints: Thoughts About Paintings Conservation*, ed. by Mark Leonard (Los Angeles: The Getty Conservation Institute, 2003), pp. 37, 76.
5. Ibid, pp. 31–39.
6. Isabelle Brajer, 'To Retouch or Not to Retouch? – Reflections on the Aesthetic Completion of Wall Paintings', *CeroArt* (June 2015). <https://doi.org/10.4000/ceroart.4619> [accessed 5 March 2023].
7. Paolo Mora, Laura Mora and Paul Philippot, 'Problems of Presentation', Reading 36 in *Historical and Philosophical Issues in the Conservation of Cultural Heritage (Readings in Conservation)*, ed. by Nicholas Stanley Price, M. Kirby Talley, Jr. and Alessandra Melucco Vaccaro (Los Angeles: Getty Conservation Institute, 1996), pp. 343–354.
8. Isabelle Brajer, 'The Simulative Retouching Method on Wall Paintings: Striving for Authenticity or Verisimilitude?', in *BRK-APROA Postprint: Reflex or Reflection?: Actors and Decision-Making in Conservation-Restoration*, November 19–20, 2009, Auditorium Hadewych Brussels (Brussels: BRK-APROA, 2009), pp. 100–109.
9. Ornella Casazza, *Il Restauro Pittorico – Nell'Unità di Metodologia* (Firenze: Nardini Editore, 1981).
10. Balkan Heritage Foundation, *Workshop for Conservation of Roman and Late Roman Pottery from Stobi (2010–2014)*, ed. by Angele Pencheva (Sofia: Balkan Heritage Foundation, National Institution Stobi, 2016).
11. Debra Hess Norris and Jennifer Jae Gutierrez, *Issues in the Conservation of Photographs* (Los Angeles: The Getty Conservation Institute, 2010), pp. 303, 379, 627–628.
12. Leonor Loureiro, Cátia Silva and Ana Catarina Rosa, 'Chromatic Reintegration of 20th Century Monochrome Photographs Showing Plain and Texture Paper Surfaces', in *Postprints of the 3rd International Meeting on Retouching of Cultural Heritage, RECH 3*, October 23–24, 2015, Porto (Porto: Escola Artística e Profissional Arvore, 2016), pp. 113–122.
13. Myriam Serck-Dewaide, 'Sixteenth-Century Antwerp-Style Altarpieces of the Church of Saint-Nicolas at Enghien and the Church of Saint-Lambert at Bouvignes, Belgium', in *Methodology for the Conservation of Polychromed Wooden Altarpieces*, ed. by Françoise Descamps (Los Angeles: The Getty Conservation Institute, 2002), pp. 20–33.
14. Adriano Reis Ramos, 'Main Altarpiece of the Cathedral of Santo Antonio, Santa Barbara, Minas Gerais, Brazil', in *Methodology for the Conservation of Polychromed Wooden Altarpieces* (Sevilla: Junta de Andalucía. Consejería de Cultura and Los Angeles: The J. Paul Getty Trust, 2002), pp. 54–65.
15. Frances Lennard, 'Preserving Image and Structure: Tapestry Conservation in Europe and the United States', *Studies in Conservation*, 51.suppl (2006), 43–53.
16. Mária Kralovánszky, 'Problems of the Second Restoration of Two General's Atillas (Military Coats) from 1848–1849', in *Conserving Textiles – Studies in Honour of Ágnes Timár-Balázsy*, ed. by István Éri (Rome: ICCROM, 2009), pp. 97–102.
17. Gerry Hedley, *Measured Opinions: Collected Papers on the Conservation of Paintings*, ed. by Caroline Villers (London: United Kingdom Institute for Conservation, 1993).
18. <www.culturalheritage.org/about-conservation/code-of-ethics> [accessed 13 February 2023].

19. <https://aiccm.org.au/wp-content/uploads/2020/01/CODE-OF-ETHICS-AND-CODE-OF-PRACTICE-Australian-Institute-for-Conservation-of-Cultural-Material-1.pdf> [accessed 13 February 2023].

20. <www.cac-accr.ca/about-us/> [accessed 13 February 2023].

21. <https://capc-acrp.ca/en/what-is-conservation/publications/code-of-ethics-and-guidance-for-practice> [accessed 13 February 2023].

22. <www.ecco-eu.org/home/ecco-documents/#___ECCO_Professional_Guidelines__> [accessed 13 February 2023].

23. <www.icon.org.uk/resources/resources-for-conservation-professionals/standards-and-ethics.html> [accessed 13 February 2023].

24. *Historical and Philosophical Issues in the Conservation of Cultural Heritage (Readings in Conservation)*, ed. by Nicholas Stanley Price, M. Kirby Talley, Jr. and Alessandra Melucco Vaccaro (Los Angeles: Getty Conservation Institute, 1996).

25. John Rushkin, 'The Lamp of Memory, I', Reading 1 in *Historical and Philosophical Issues in the Conservation of Cultural Heritage (Readings in Conservation)*, ed. by Nicholas Stanley Price, M. Kirby Talley, Jr. and Alessandra Melucco Vaccaro (Los Angeles: Getty Conservation Institute, 1996), p. 42.

26. Cesare Brandi, *Theory of Restoration*, English edn, Instituto Centrale per il Restauro (Firenze: Naridini Editore, 2005).

27. Cesare Brandi, 'The Cleaning of Pictures in Relation to Patina, Varnish, and Glazes', in *Historical and Philosophical Issues in the Conservation of Cultural Heritage (Readings in Conservation)*, ed. by Nicholas Stanley Price, M. Kirby Talley, Jr. and Alessandra Melucco Vaccaro (Los Angeles: Getty Conservation Institute, 1996), pp. 380–393.

28. Cesare Brandi, 'Restoration with Regard to the Aesthetic Case', in *Theory of Restoration*, English edn, Instituto Centrale per il Restauro (Firenze: Naridini Editore, 2005), p. 74.

29. John Richardson, 'Crimes Against the Cubists', Reading 18 in *Historical and Philosophical Issues in the Conservation of Cultural Heritage (Readings in Conservation)*, ed. by Nicholas Stanley Price, M. Kirby Talley, Jr. and Alessandra Melucco Vaccaro (Los Angeles: Getty Conservation Institute, 1996), pp. 185–192.

30. Albert Albano, 'Art in Transition', Reading 17 in *Historical and Philosophical Issues in the Conservation of Cultural Heritage (Readings in Conservation)*, ed. by Nicholas Stanley Price, M. Kirby Talley, Jr. and Alessandra Melucco Vaccaro (Los Angeles: Getty Conservation Institute, 1996), pp. 176–184.

31. Burlington Index, 'The Burlington Magazine and the National Gallery Cleaning Controversy (1947–1963)'. <https://burlingtonindex.wordpress.com/2015/07/11/the-burlington-magazine-and-the-national-gallery-cleaning-controversy-1947-1963/> [accessed 14 March 2023].

32. D. Bomford and S. Staniforth, 'Wax-Resin Lining and Colour Change: An Evaluation', *National Gallery Technical Bulletin*, 5 (1981), 58–65.

33. J. Ashley-Smith, 'A Role for Bespoke Codes of Ethics', in *ICOM Committee for Conservation 18th Triennial Meeting Copenhagen Preprints*, ed. by Janet Bridgland (Paris: International Congress of Museums, 2017), paper no. 1742.

34. *Personal Viewpoints: Thoughts About Paintings Conservation*, ed. by Mark Leonard (Los Angeles: The Getty Conservation Institute, 2003).

35. Laramie Hickey-Friedman, 'A Review of Ultra-Violet Light and Examination Techniques', in *Objects Specialty Group Postprints*, Vol. 9, ed. by Virginia Greene

and Patricia Griffin (Washington, DC: The American Institute for Conservation of Historic & Artistic Works, 2002), pp. 161–168.

36. Hao Tian, Xiaotian Zeng, Jianbo Guo, Liang Qu and Kunlong Chen, 'X-ray Computed Tomography Reveals Special Casting Techniques Used with Unusual Bronze Objects Unearthed from the Sanxingdui Site', *Advances in Archaeomaterials*, 3.1 (2022), 28-33.

37. Jane Bassett, *The Craftsman Revealed – Adriaen de Vries: Sculptor in Bronze* (Los Angeles: The Getty Conservation Institute, 2008).

38. Joyce Hill Stoner, 'Changing Approaches in Art Conservation: 1925 to the Present', in *Scientific Examination of Art: Modern Techniques in Conservation and Analysis*, National Research Council (Washington, DC: The National Academies Press, 2005), pp. 40–57.

39. J. R. J. van Asperen de Boer, 'Reflectography of Paintings Using an Infrared Vidicon Television System', *Studies in Conservation*, 14 (1969), 96–118.

40. J. R. J. van Asperen de Boer, 'Infrared Reflectography: A Contribution to the Examination of Earlier European Paintings' (doctoral thesis, University of Amsterdam, 1970).

41. Molly Faries, 'Analytical Capabilities of Infrared Reflectography: An Art Historian's Perspective', in *Scientific Examination of Art: Modern Techniques in Conservation and Analysis* (Washington, DC: National Academies Press, 2005), pp. 87–104.

42. John K. Delaney, Giorgio Trumpy, Marie Didier, Paola Ricciardi and Kathryn A. Dooley, 'A High Sensitivity, Low Noise and High Spatial Resolution Multi-Band Infrared Reflectography Camera for the Study of Paintings and Works on Paper', *Heritage Science*, 5 (2017), 32.

43. B. D. Cullity, 'Chemical Analysis by Absorption', in *Elements of X-ray Diffraction* (Reading: Addison-Wesley Publishing Company, 1956), pp. 423–430.

44. Industry Tap into News, 'A Brief History of X-Ray Fluorescence'. <www.industrytap.com/a-brief-history-of-x-ray-fluorescence/56091> [accessed 16 March 2023].

45. Francesca Caterina Izzo, *20th Century Artist's Oil Paints; A Chemical-Physical Survey* (doctoral thesis, Università Ca' Foscari Venezia, 2011), pp. 140–141.

46. Birgit Anne van Driel, *Titanium White, Friend or Foe?* (doctoral thesis, Delft University of Technology, 2018).

47. Edward Cloutis, Alesha MacKay, Lief Norman and Doug Goltz, 'Identification of Historic Artists' Pigments Using Spectral Reflectance and X-Ray Diffraction Properties I. Iron Oxide and Oxy-Hydroxide-Rich Pigments', *Journal of Near Infrared Spectroscopy*, 24.1 (2016). <https://doi.org/10.1255/jnirs.1198>

48. Elena Pratali, 'Zinc Oxide Ground in 19th and 20th Century Oil Paintings and Their Role in Pictue Degradation Processes', *CeroArt* (2013). <https://doi.org/10.4000/ceroart.3207>

49. W. Wei, H. van Keulen and M. Geldof, *Unpublished Research* (Amersfoort: Cultural Heritage Agency of the Netherlands, 2016).

50. Michael R. Schilling, 'Paint Media Analysis', in *Scientific Examination of Art: Modern Techniques in Conservation and Analysis* (Washington, DC: National Academies Press, 2005), pp. 186–205.

51. Eugenia Geddes da Filicaia, Richard P. Evershed and David A. Peggie, 'Review of Recent Advances on the Use of Mass Spectrometry Techniques for the Study

of Organic Materials in Painted Artworks', *Analytica Chimica Acta*, 1246 (2023). <https://doi.org/10.1016/j.aca.2022.340575>

52. Robin J. H. Clark, 'Raman Microscopy in the Identification of Pigments on Manuscripts and Other Artwork', in *Scientific Examination of Art: Modern Techniques in Conservation and Analysis* (Washington, DC: National Academies Press, 2005), pp. 162–185.

53. Communication Unit Synchrotron SOLEIL, *Highlights 2018*, Publicity Booklet, Jean Daillant, director (Gyf-Sur-Yvette: SOLEIL, 2019).

54. Simona Quartieri, 'Synchrotron Radiation in Art, Archaeology and Cultural Heritage', in *Synchrotron Radiation*, ed. by Settimio Mobilio, Federico Boscherini and Carlo Meneghini (Berlin: Springer-Verlag, 2015), Chapter 26, pp. 677–695.

55. Jean-Claude Dran, 'Accelerators in Art and Archaeology', in *Proceedings of 8th European Particle Accelerator Conference EPAC*, June 3–7, Paris, ed. by Terence Garvey and others (Geneva: European Physical Society, 2002), pp. 124-128.

56. Catherine Dejoie, Pierre-Olivier Autran, Pierre Bordet, Andy N. Fitch, Pauline Martinetto, Philippe Sciau, Nobumichi Tamura and Jonathan Wright, 'X-ray Diffraction and Heterogeneous Materials: An Adaptive Crystallography Approach', *Comptes Rendus Physique*, 19 (2018), 553–560.

57. Dudley Creagh, 'Synchrotron Radiation and It Use in Art, Archaeometry, and Cultural Heritage Studies', in *Physical Techniques in the Study of Art, Archaeology and Cultural Heritage*, ed. by Dudley Creagh and David Bradley (Amsterdam: Elsevier B.V., 2007), Chapter 1, pp. 1–95.

58. Cecily M. Grzywacz, *Tools in Conservation: Monitoring for Gaseous Pollutants in Museum Environments* (Los Angeles: The Getty Conservation Institute, 2006).

59. Oscar Chiantori and Tommaso Poli, 'Indoor Air Quality in Museum Display Cases: Volatile Emissions, Materials Contributions, Impacts', *Atmosphere*, 12.3 (2021), 364-382.

60. *Climate for Collections: Standards and Uncertainties*, ed. by Jonathan Ashley-Smith, Andreas Burmester and Melanie Bauernfeind (London: Archetype Publications, 2013).

61. Agnes Brokerhof, Bart Ankersmit and Frank Ligterink, *Risk Management for Collections* (Amsterdam: Cultural Heritage Agency of the Netherlands, 2017).

62. Robert Waller, 'Collection Risk Assessment', in *Preventive Conservation: Collection Storage*, ed. by Lisa Elkin and Christopher A. Norris (New York: Society for the Preservation of Natural History; American Institute for Conservation of Historic and Artistic Works; Smithsonian Institution; The George Washington University Museum Studies Program, 2019), pp. 59–90.

63. *Assessing Museum Collections Collection Valuation in Six Steps* (Amersfoort: Cultural Heritage Agency of the Netherlands, 2014).

64. Roslyn Russel and Kylie Winkworth, *Significance 2.0: A Guide to Assessing he Significance of Collections* (Rundle Mall: Collections Council of Australia, 2009).

65. Robert L. Feller, *Accelerated Aging: Photochemical and Thermal Aspects* (Los Angeles: The J. Paul Getty Trust, 1994).

66. <https://dictionary.cambridge.org/dictionary/english/innovation> [accessed 27 December 2022].

2 Original appearance, perception, and eye-tracking

In the previous chapter, the background for the development of conservation science and further innovations was discussed. Much of this development revolved around the requirements of conservation codes of ethics, in particular, the requirement to make well-informed decisions and to protect the original materials of an object. Implicit in these codes is that not following them and "ruining" an object will make it impossible to ever bring it anywhere back to its original state or appearance. The underlying belief is that conservation science can provide objective scientific results to support conservation decisions. However, the results of a conservation decision and treatment (or not) ultimately rest on what the conservator and other heritage professionals see.

This chapter will take a brief look at what it is that people see and perceive in a work of art. The chapter begins with a short discussion of the meaning of originality, authenticity and original appearance. This is followed by a brief overview of current views on the perception of works of art and cultural heritage. Finally, the innovative technique of eye-tracking is introduced, showing that the general public does not necessarily see what heritage professionals think they should see. In all of this subjective uncertainty lies the question as to what objective conservation science is producing in the way of innovative results and what kind of decision-making it is supporting, if any.

2.1 The search for originality, authenticity, and original appearance

The protection of original material, or the protection of the original object and its appearance, is a concept recognized by anyone who has become attached to some object which has a direct relationship to some event or person in the past. The reader has certainly heard of a story where a woman loses her wedding ring down the drain. Her husband offers to buy her another one and is left speechless as she furiously storms out of the room. It was not *the* ring which he had put on her finger at the wedding. Then there is the age-old question of what one thing one would rescue in the event of a fire at home. The answer is very often the family photograph album.

DOI: 10.4324/9781003217800-2

Original thus indicates something physical. In fact, as was discussed by this author [1], something is "original," according to the dictionary definition, if it is a unique object or the first of many similar objects made by the maker. The "original" materials are the materials that the maker used in making the "original" object. However, original for many art historians and the public also implies how an object appeared when it was first made, straight off the easel or workbench. In this use of the term "original," one is then expanding the term to not only include the materials the maker used, but also the maker's original intent within the context of the times, and the places where the maker lived, work, traveled, or otherwise frequented.

On the other hand, something is "authentic" in the dictionary sense of the word if it gives the observer the feeling that it is original [1]. One generally speaks of a copy or reproduction of an original object as being authentic if it provides someone the feeling that the original would provide. Aside from not being original, the replacement ring which the husband offered his wife does not at all have that feeling of authenticity. On the other hand, one can certainly argue that many original works of art have lost meaning and authenticity since they have long since been taken out of the context which may have influenced the artists' intent, and the context in which they were originally displayed.

Conservators also speak of materials used to restore an object as being original materials, that is, chemically the same as what the maker used or, better, coming from the maker's own workshop. In this way one comes closer to the artist's intent, and the restoration is more authentic. At some point, however, one begins to run into the Theseus ship paradox, questioning whether an object which, over time and many treatments, has had all of its components replaced with "original" materials, is still the original. Some people would at least say that it would be authentic.

The definition and role of artist's or maker's intent in the question of the originality and authenticity of a work of art is also a subject of immense debate. There are a number of considerations when it comes to the conservation of a work of art. Dykstra [2] lists 11 variations of what artist's intent entails:

1. biographical motives
2. aims versus outcomes
3. expression in media
4. inherent creative spirit
5. the artist's speaking
6. the artist's telling
7. the artist's expressive character
8. the artwork's aesthetic expression
9. the artwork's appeal for reference and characterization
10. the artwork's aesthetic agency
11. moral effect of the artwork.

Of those, only numbers 2 and 3 have a direct relationship with artist's materials and thus with scientific analysis, as discussed in the previous chapter. The others are, simply put, purely subjective in nature. If one considers the role of conservation science in this sense, it is not particularly large, and even numbers 2 and 3 do carry a considerable amount of subjectivity.

In fact, one could argue that the core of the cleaning controversy lay in those two parts of artist intent. Dykstra further notes that science has been used since the 19th century as a basis for art historical and conservation decisions based on the "confidence that a measure of scientific objectivity would dispel any perceptions of art restoration as an entirely interpretive and unrestrained process" [3]. However, during the National Gallery controversy, this positivist attitude had equally strong resistance from, among others, Cesare Brandi and Ernst Gombrich, arguing that technically driven conservation decisions do not do justice to artists' intent. Brandi argued that one must leave the patina of an object as part of the history of the object which is closer to the original hand of the artist [4], while Gombrich argued, quoting Dykstra, "that paintings should be restored with a comparative and discerning eye toward their faded colors, their characteristic patina, and inevitable decay" [5]. It is clear, that even the modern field of technical art history, which uses scientific analysis as the basis for determining the history and original appearance of works of art, is ultimately driven by subjective interpretation. Philippot recognized that conservation decisions such as removing varnish are a question of taste, and that "The conservator's objectivity is, in effect, illusory, since it is bought at the price of substituting a merely material criterion for critical judgement" [6].

To make the debate more interesting, it is noted that Baxandall takes issue with the concept of even trying to determine artist's intent in interpreting pictures, "The most obvious and threatening of these is the debate, conducted mainly in the context of literature, about whether reconstruction of the maker's intention is a proper part of interpretation of a work of art" [7]. He notes further, "The relation between period art criticism and what we are doing at present is in any case complex. The appearance of art criticism of an idea from an extraneous universe does not necessarily mean it was actively in play in the painters' intention: it does mean it was possible in the period for someone to make the connection – a necessary but not sufficient condition for its use in explanation" [8]. And finally, "For some time two related issues have been hanging around this discussion of intention. One is the question of how far we are really going to penetrate into the intentional fabric of painters living in cultures or periods remote from our own. The other is the question of whether we can in any sense or degree verify or validate our explanations" [9].

In recent years, the meanings of the terms original and authentic have become confused in the art historical and conservation literature as authors twist semantics in order to make some point about decision-making in the preservation of cultural heritage [1]. This is evident, for example, in articles published in two conference proceedings on authenticity [10, 11], where various authors used different and sometimes inconsistent definitions of the concepts of "authenticity" and "original object," as well as the concept of the "real thing." In *Contemporary Theory of Conservation* by Muñoz-Viñas, the words "original" and "authentic/authenticity" are not mentioned very often. However, in his discussion of objectivity and subjectivity in conservation decision-making, the emphasis is more on concepts of the "nature of an object," the fact that there are only "true" objects and no "false" objects, and the concept of a "real" object [12]. At the end of the chapter, he notes, "As the tautological argument proves, relating the authenticity of an object to its original condition (or to any other past or presumed condition) is an entirely subjective choice." However, the discussion leading to that point involves the use of the terms "authentic," "original," "real," and "true," which, at least for this author, makes it hard to follow what the difference between the terms is. A further question of what one is dealing with when one starts digitizing works of art will be discussed in Chapter 5.

The already confusing use of the terms authentic and original is made all the more confusing by the word "authentication," which in the art world as well as in other professions means the verification that a work of art, in particular, a unique work, was actually made by the maker it was attributed to, that is, it is "original." Be that as it may, for the purposes of this book, the terms original/originality will refer to the material object as it was made by the artist, and the terms authentic/authenticity will refer to the feelings about an object. This leaves us then with the question of what the role of conservation science and, in particular, innovation in art conservation is in what people see in a work of art.

2.2   Looking at and perceiving art

The answer to the question of what works of art, in particular, paintings, originally looked like is quite complex. On the one hand, it depends on what the artists intended, and thus on how they worked, their choice of materials, form, and color, and the context in which they worked. On the other hand, it depends on how people originally viewed and perceived the works in their original context, and how that has changed through the (hundreds of) years.

Over the centuries, a vast literature has been written by art historians, who have conducted extensive research in order to explain how art developed from prehistoric times to the present, and have used this information to teach the general public how art is to be viewed and interpreted. This literature ranges from classical tomes on the entire history of art such as H.W. Janson's *History of Art* [13 and the following editions] and professional literature on all imaginable areas of art and art history, to coffee table books and catalogues, and multi-volume series on artists for the general public.

Given the amount of careful and detailed research needed to write such histories, it is not surprising that many people have considered such literature to be objective sources of information about art, artists, and artists' intent. Almost every museum has, if not a well-equipped and staffed education department, access to trained docents to teach visitors all that they need to know about the basics of the art in the museum's collection. They also set up programs for schools and adult education classes to provide even more advanced knowledge. Conservation science and recent innovations are popular, especially for the larger well-financed museums, for providing the public with fascinating details about how an artist worked and created a work of art, and digital images of how the work may have appeared before it had aged or otherwise degraded to its current condition.

However, in the past several decades, a number of art historians and cultural heritage professionals have begun to question this "professional" way of looking at art or cultural heritage in general, and whether art history is as objective as it is made out to be. In fact, Baxandall questions what it is that art historians are doing when they describe a picture.

It seems to me absurd to claim that there is a proper way to look at pictures.

[7]

We do not explain pictures: we explain remarks about pictures – or rather, we explain pictures only in so far as we have considered them under some verbal description or specification. . . . Every evolved explanation of a picture includes or implies an elaborate description of that picture. The explanation of the picture then in its turn becomes part of the larger description of the picture, a way of describing things about it that would be difficult to describe in another way.

[14]

More recently, Laurajane Smith even questions what it is that heritage professionals tell people, that is, what they should consider important and valuable enough to enjoy, learn from, and preserve [15]. This "authorized heritage discourse" (AHD), as she calls it, is something that has been developed and passed on through the years by an elite group of professionals who are supposedly the only people properly trained and qualified to decide what can be considered important cultural heritage. This discourse is certainly present in the world of art and art conservation, as the literature is flooded with new research on yet another important work of art which viewers are told should be seen in a certain way. The AHD essentially says that one has to be trained to be able to "enjoy," "understand," or at least "accept" art.

The previous brief discussion focuses on the context of art and art history, and how people view or, rather, how they "are supposed to view" art. The discussion becomes more interesting when one considers what people perceive when they view a work of art, that is, what happens after what one is supposed to see is passed on from the human eye into the brain. As will be discussed in more detail in Section 3.3, there is still no clear understanding of human visual perception, let alone of any of the other four sensorial types of perception.

How people perceive works of art is only one of the many issues confronting researchers in the field of perception in general (see, e.g., [16, 17].) It is made all the more complex because of possible differences between the viewing and perception of a real object or landscape, and the viewing and perception of a figurative work of art depicting the object or landscape. E.H. Gombrich was one of the pioneers in modern-day research into the perception of art. In his well-known book, *Art and Illusion*, he discusses the many issues that artists face in trying to produce a representation of nature which is convincing (or illusory) to the human mind [18] and that it is possible to make a picture that looks like the real thing. This became a subject of philosophical debate with J.J. Gibson, who argued that reality and a picture of it are two different things. A picture, for example, provides direct information about an object or scene so that the viewer knows what the whole looks like, while, Gombrich argued, a picture of an object or scene is always different from the real object or scene (see, e.g., [19, 20]).

In recent years, there have been considerable scientific efforts to help explain perception in art (see, e.g., [21, 22]). This includes, for example, geometric studies on how reflections are (mis)represented in paintings [23], the use of geometric analysis to determine facial recognition [24], or understanding how viewers approach abstract works of art [25]. Related to these studies, Jan Koenderink's group at the University of Utrecht has performed considerable work on understanding the perception of three-dimensional relief in two-dimensional pictures (e.g., [26, 27]).

Given the wealth and subjectivity of art historical information, and the lack of understanding of human perception, especially in the case of viewing art, one is certainly justified in asking what a viewer is doing when looking at works of art in a museum. How long does the average visitor look at a painting, and what is she or he really looking at in the work? This varies quite widely, but most visitors are certainly not spending the hours which an art historian or conservator or conservation scientist spends in front of a work of art. And do they see what professionals think they should see and worry about?

2.3   Eye-tracking

In the previous section, the question was discussed as to how viewers look at and perceive art, or at least, how art historians and other heritage professionals think they should see art. It was seen in recent years, that this "authorized heritage discourse" on the perception of art is being increasingly challenged.

Support for these challenges is growing, thanks to an innovative technique known as eye-tracking.

Eye-tracking makes use of an instrument which allows researchers to follow the eye movements of subjects. In that way, they can determine how they look at an object or, more generally, at their surroundings. Eye-tracking follows the chronological order in which they look at particular features. The technique can also determine which features attract their attention based on how long their eyes rest on a certain point in a scene.

Baxandall actually tried to describe how the observer views an object before eye-tracking was developed. He wrote:

The gait of the eye, in fact, changes in the course of inspecting an object. At first, we are getting our bearings, it moves not only more quickly but more widely; presently it settles down to movements at a rate of something like four or five a second and shifts of something like three to five degrees.
[28]

A basic eye-tracking system is shown in Fig. 2.1. The eye-tracker is positioned in front of a computer screen, which will be viewed by the test subject. The tracker sends an infrared beam to the human pupils, which is then reflected by the cornea. The reflection depends on the orientation of the eye. The change of the reflected beam as the eye (pupil) moves is detected by a high-resolution camera. With proper calibration, this allows the eye-tracker to precisely follow what the viewer is looking at, and in what order. It also determines how long the eyes rest at any point, presenting these as so-called heat maps. Such a stationary system is used, for example, in marketing to determine how people look at websites. A more advanced version of eye-tracking makes use of sensors built into eyeglass frames. The subject thus moves around in the environment of interest. This advanced version is also used for marketing purposes to determine, for example, how people shop in stores and what attracts their attention. It is also used in industry, for example, for safety design by observing how people drive a car or perform risky tasks in the workplace.

Typical results for an eye-tracking test conducted by the author and one of his students on a computer image of a painting are shown in Fig. 2.2 [29]. The results for three of the participants, art conservation students, are shown in a, b, and c. It can be seen that the three subjects do not look at the painting in the same way. This is evident in the different chronological viewing routes (numbers) and the different locations in the painting which attracted their attention (larger circles).

Another interesting experiment was conducted by the Free University of Amsterdam (VU), comparing how children and adults look at paintings [30]. The subjects were fitted with eye-tracking equipment mounted on eyeglass frames, so that they could freely move around the paintings as normally as possible.

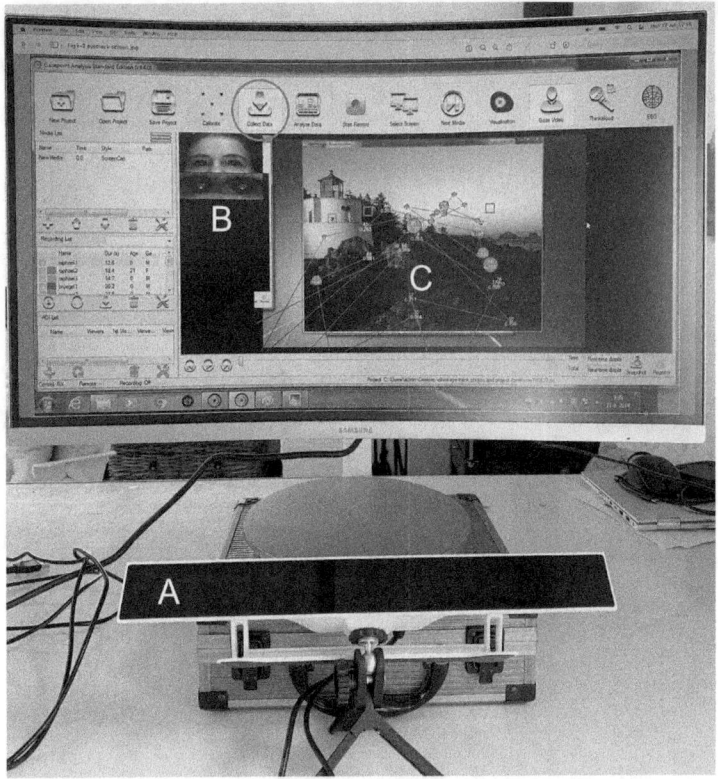

Fig. 2.1 Stationary eye-tracking system for use in front of computer screen

A – eye-tracker

B – calibration screen

C – scene being observed

The results showed that if allowed to look at paintings freely, that is, with no introduction, children focused more on salient features of the paintings, that is, those which grabbed their attention. How they viewed the paintings was determined by so-called bottom-up factors, that is, by the physical environment. However, adults concentrated more on other low-salient features, that is, features that do not initially stick out. They appear to have concentrated on things that they had some knowledge of in some way or another. This is known as a top-down attentional process, "determined by goals, intentions and interpretation of the observer" [30]. When the children and adults were then read a description of the painting, the differences in the eye-tracking results were reduced significantly, showing that previous knowledge affects how paintings are looked at.

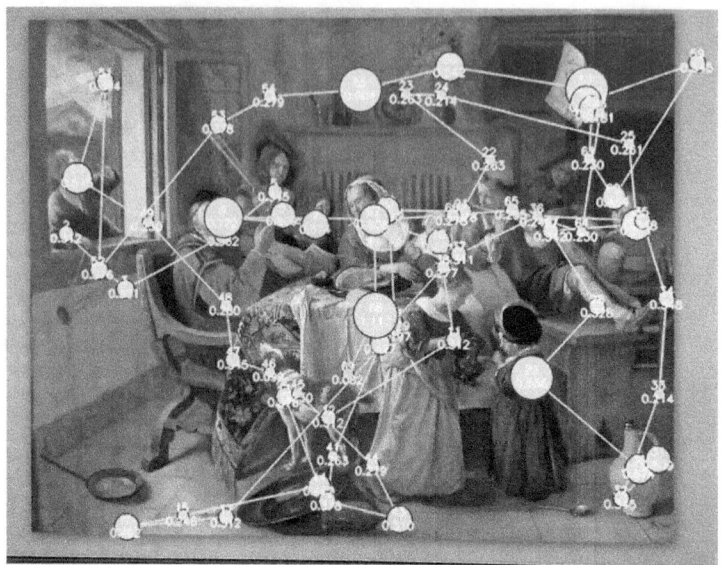

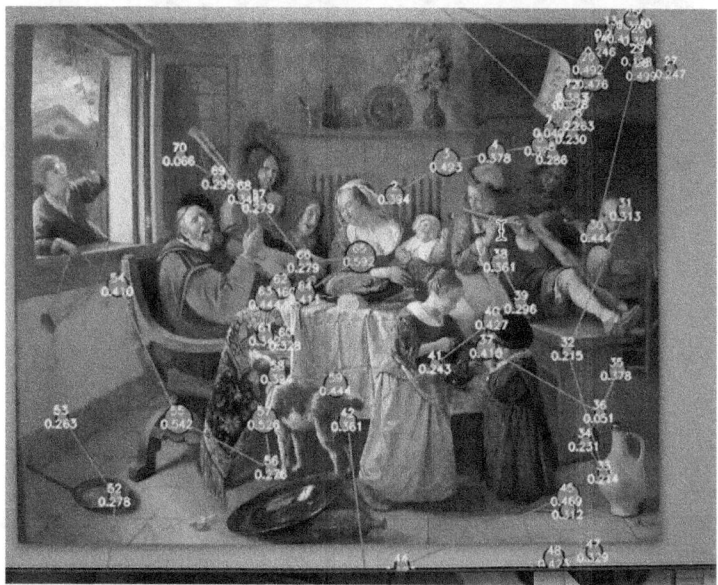

Fig. 2.2 Results for eye-tracking tests showing three participants look at a painting in different ways [29]. The integers indicate the chronological order of viewing, and the size of the circles indicates how long the participant's eyes rested on that particular location. (Painting: "Merry Family" (1668) by Jan Steen)

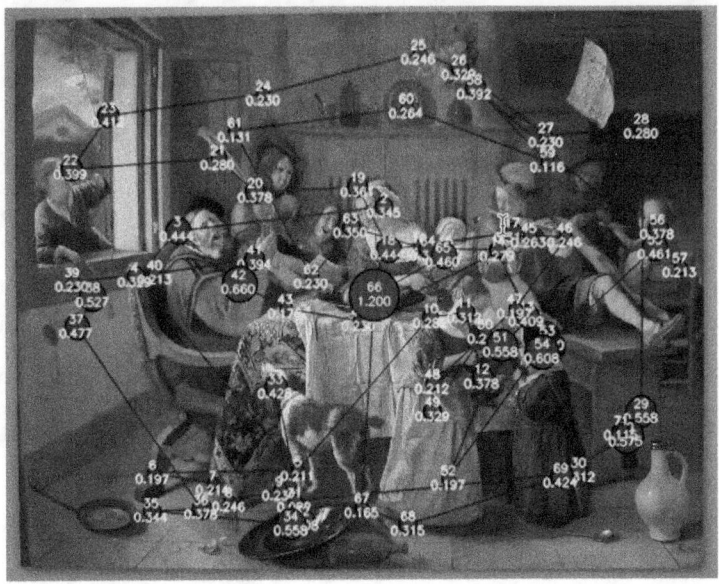

Fig. 2.2 (Continued)

Rosenberg and Klein also observed that visitors to museums tend to use top-down information to look at paintings [31]. However, they also noted that the typical visitor only looks at a painting for less than 30 seconds, quoting work that shows that this is far less than what an art historian considers necessary [32]. Furthermore, they found that how the public looks at paintings is not at all that predicted by so-called art historian experts. "Eyes do not follow any line of composition in a continuous manner, nor do beholders scan paintings from top to bottom or left to right continuously" [33]. It was noted that prior knowledge changed how one looks at a painting. For example, when looking at simple paintings, eye movement patterns were similar between experts and non-experts, but for a complex painting, eye movements were different in the beginning. The interpretation of the results was that nonexperts need more time to understand the structure of the painting. Instructions, aesthetic texts, painting titles, and speaking were shown to affect the results.

The eye-tracking research by Pepperell and Ishai, mentioned previously [25], also indicates that prior knowledge affects how people read paintings, in particular, reading so-called indeterminate artworks or, put more simply, abstract art. "Visual indeterminacy occurs when an image or a scene is structured in such a way as to defy immediate or easy recognition." This is not to be confused with optical illusions. When studying how people viewed Cubist paintings, they found that a short training helped viewers better recognize objects if a meaningful title was given to a painting before they saw it, instead of "untitled."

The use of eye-tracking has also been introduced in art conservation. The technique was used to help with the restoration of what had been considered a "total-loss" painting, John Martin's *Destruction of Pompeii and Herculaeum*," which was badly damaged during flooding in Tate Gallery in 1928, resulting in a large lacuna covering roughly one-third of the picture [34]. When the painting was reexamined years later, it was thought that it could be repaired. Virtual images were made of various ways to fill in the lacuna. This included what is known as an artistic, illusionistic, or realistic inpainting based on a later version of the painting, as well as the "standard" use of a neutral color considered not to be distracting. Eye-tracking showed again that people looked at salient features, the volcano itself and the burning city below. The border of the lacuna was near the volcano eruption and did distract them initially, but they then focused on the volcano and the city. An interesting point was that the public preferred the realistic or abstract infill as opposed to something neutral, even though conservation theories and codes of ethics warn against realistic infilling. The audience did want to see what the whole painting could have looked like.

Before reading further, the reader is requested to look at Fig. 2.3 (also on next page) and answer this question, "Which version do you prefer?"

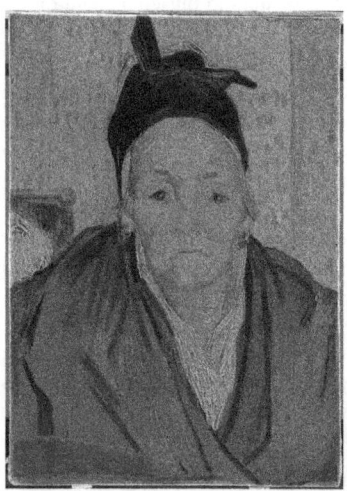 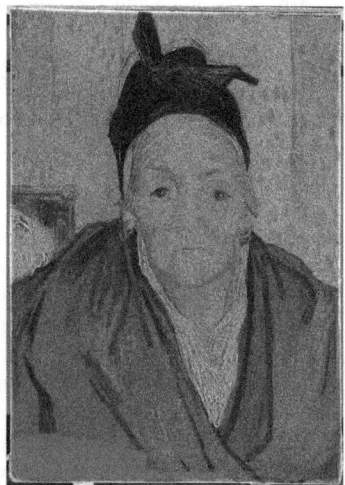

Fig. 2.3 Which version do you prefer?

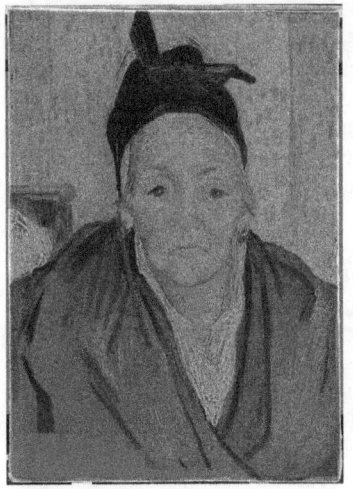 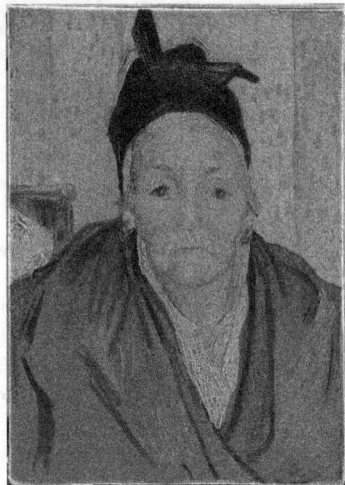

Fig. 2.3 (Continued)

This preference for a realistic infill was confirmed by a perception study without eye-tracking equipment, which was conducted by the author and one of his students. This study could be considered to be a negative eye-tracking experiment, that is, determining what subjects do not see. The study was conducted with a conservator of one of Vincent van Gogh's paintings, the *Old Woman of Arles* [35]. The painting had a lacuna in the lower left-hand corner of the painting, probably damaged sometime early in its history, but Van Gogh does not write about it. It was retouched with neutral gray paint some time before the 1970s, a retouch which was recently considered to be in poor condition and in need of redoing [36]. Current interpretations of conservation codes of ethics require redoing the retouch in a neutral gray, and that an artistic infilling is considered not done. This was also the conclusion of a master's thesis on the subject, with the additional suggestion that the painting be shown unframed so that the history (damage) of the in-painting could be clearly seen [36].

In order to have an idea of what a retouch would look like, it was first performed virtually using Photoshop™. The research scientist doing the work, the author, actually found the gray, which had been chosen by the conservator, to be rather garish, at least on the computer screen, and suggested using a blue-green which would better match the dark blue and green shades in the woman's coat. A student also produced an artistic fill-in using the cloning and stamping functions of Photoshop™. Four versions were presented to the general public at an exhibition in the form of posters, and on one PowerPoint™

slide on a large projection screen to two conference audiences – one of mostly conservators and the other of more conservation scientists. Without any introduction, they were merely asked to choose which version they preferred. These were the ones shown in Fig. 2.3. After the vote, they (and you, the reader) were then asked to be honest and were asked whether they had even noticed that the question of preference had to do with the lower left-hand corner. An overwhelming majority of the participants admitted not even looking there.

And indeed, why would they? When an artist paints a portrait and someone looks at it, it is pretty safe to assume that the viewer will be looking at the face and the immediate surroundings of the person portraited, and not at one of the corners of the painting. In agreement with the eye-tracking results of Rosenberg and Klein, as well as those of Massaro et al. [37] using paintings with an obvious human subject, the results on the *Old Woman of Arles* clearly show that viewers concentrate on the faces of the painted subject [35].

Other eye-tracking and perception tests conducted by the author and his students confirm that the audience does not see art the way professionals think they should. For example, videos of (unidentifiable) people visiting contemporary art installations show that they rarely spend more than a few seconds, at the most, a half a minute, in front of such objects. Perception tests, in particular, innovative eye-tracking techniques, therefore clearly show that the general public is not looking at what heritage professionals think are important and think that people should be looking at. In the following chapters, this issue will be examined more closely in relation to recent and ongoing innovations in conservation science dealing with original appearance and color of art.

2.4   Summary of Chapter 2

In this chapter, the subjectivity behind conservation decisions was examined. Though originality and authenticity play a major role in conservation decisions, it was shown that the use of the terms in the conservation and art historical literature has drifted far from their dictionary definitions. This has muddled the discussion of what the result of a conservation treatment should be and what people should see in a restored work of art. However, the question of what people should see is also up for debate. Traditional heritage professionals claim to know how one should view works of art, but an increasing number of their colleagues are beginning to question this top-down attitude. Furthermore, perception studies, including the use of eye-tracking, show that people do not view works of art the way heritage professionals think they do or should. This then leads to the question where innovative technology is leading art conservation to in terms of bringing back originality, or at least, authenticity, to the appearance of a work of art. This will be considered in the following three chapters, using color science and digital imaging technology as an example.

References

1. William (Bill) Wei, 'Authenticity and Originality, Objectivity and Subjectivity in Conservation Decision-Making – or Is It Just a Matter of Taste?', *Studies in Conservation*, 67.1–2 (2022), 15–20.
2. Steven W. Dykstra, 'The Artist's Intentions and the Intentional Fallacy in Fine Arts Conservation', *Journal of the American Institute for Conservation*, 35.3 (1996), 197–281.
3. Ibid, p. 201.
4. Ibid, p. 202.
5. Ibid.
6. Paul Philippot, 'The Idea of Patina and the Cleaning of Paintings', Reading 39 in *Historical and Philosophical Issues in the Conservation of Cultural Heritage (Readings in Conservation)*, ed. by Nicholas Stanley Price, M. Kirby Talley, Jr. and Alessandra Melucco Vaccaro (Los Angeles: Getty Conservation Institute, 1996), pp. 372–376.
7. M. Baxandall, *Patterns of Intention: On the Historical Explanation of Pictures* (New Haven: Yale University Press, 1985), p. vi.
8. M. Baxandall, *Patterns of Intention: On the Historical Explanation of Pictures* (New Haven: Yale University Press, 1985), pp. 80–81.
9. M. Baxandall, *Patterns of Intention: On the Historical Explanation of Pictures* (New Haven: Yale University Press, 1985), p. 105.
10. *Art and Conservation and Authenticities: Material, Concept, Context*, ed. By E. Hermens and T. Fiske (London: Archetype Publications, 2009).
11. *Authenticity and Replication – The 'Real Thing' in Art and Conservation*, ed. By R. Gordon, E. Hermens and F. Lennard (London: Archetype Publications, 2014).
12. Salvador Muñoz-Viñas, 'The Decline of Truth and Objectivity', in *Contemporary Theory of Conservation* (London: Routledge, 2005), Chapter 4, p. 106.
13. H. W. Janson, *History of Art*, 2nd edn (Englewood Cliffs: Prentice-Hall, 1977).
14. M. Baxandall, *Patterns of Intention: On the Historical Explanation of Pictures* (New Haven: Yale University Press, 1985), p. 1.
15. Laurajane Smith, *Uses of Heritage* (London: Routledge, 2006).
16. Stanley Coren, Lawrence M. Ward and James T. Enns, *Sensation and Perception*, 5th edn (Fort Worth: Harcourt Brace College Publishers, 1999).
17. Nicholas J. Wade and Michael Swanston, *Visual Perception – An Introduction* (London: Routledge, 1991).
18. Ernst Gombrich, *Art & Illusion: A Study in the Psychology of Pictorial Representation*, 6th edn (New York: Phaidon Press, 2002).
19. James J. Gibson, 'The Information Available in Pictures', *Leonardo*, 4 (1971), 27–35.
20. Ernst H. Gombrich (with James J. Gibson and Rudolf Arnheim), 'Exchange of Letters', *Leonardo*, 4 (1971), 195–203.
21. Baingio Pinna, 'Art as a Scientific Object: Toward a Visual Science of Art', in *Art and Perception – Towards a Visual Science of Art*, ed. by Baingio Pinna, Parts 1 and 2 (Leiden: Koninklijke Brill NV, 2008), p. 5.
22. *Art, Aesthetics, and the Brain*, ed. by Joseph P. Huston, Marcos Nadal, Francisco Mora, Luigi F. Agnati and Camilo Jose Cela Conde (Oxford: Oxford University Press, 2015).

23. Patrick Cavanagh, Jessica Chao and Dina Wang, 'Reflections in Art', in *Art and Perception – Towards a Visual Science of Art*, ed. by Baingio Pinna, Part 2 (Leiden: Koninklijke Brill NV, 2008), pp. 93–102.
24. Benjamin J. Balas and Pawan Sinha, 'Portraits and Perception: Configural Information in Creating and Recognizing Face Images', in *Art and Perception – Towards a Visual Science of Art*, ed. by Baingio Pinna, Part 1 (Leiden: Koninklijke Brill NV, 2008), pp. 203–219.
25. Robert C. Pepperell and Alumit Ishai, 'Indeterminate Artworks and the Human Brain', in *Art, Aesthetics, and the Brain*, ed. by Joseph P. Huston and others (Oxford: Oxford University Press, 2015), pp. 143–157.
26. Jan J. Koenderink, Andrea J. van Doorn, Chris Christou and Joseph S. Lappin, 'Shape Constancy in Pictorial Relief', in *Object Representation in Computer Vision II* (Berlin: Springer-Verlag, 1996), pp. 151–164.
27. Jan J. Koenderink, Andrea J. van Doorn and Johan Wagemans, 'Part and Whole in Pictorial Relief', *i-Perception*, 6.6 (2015), 1–21.
28. M. Baxandall, *Patterns of Intention: On the Historical Explanation of Pictures* (New Haven: Yale University Press, 1985), pp. 3–4.
29. W. (Bill) Wei and Olivia Barry, *Unpublished Research* (Cultural Heritage Agency of the Netherlands, 2018).
30. Francesco Walker, Berno Bucker, Nicola C. Anderson, Daniel Schreij and Jan Theeuwes, 'Looking at Paintings in the Vincent van Gogh Museum: Eye Movement Patterns of Children and Adults', *PLoS One*, 12.6 (2017). <https://doi.org/10.1371/journal.pone.0178912>
31. Raphael Rosenberg and Christoph Klein, 'The Moving Eye of the Beholder: Eye Tracking and the Perception of Paintings', in *Art, Aesthetics, and the Brain*, ed. by Joseph P. Huston and others (Oxford: Oxford University Press, 2015), Chapter 5, pp. 79–108.
32. Ibid, pp. 89–90.
33. Ibid, p. 94.
34. Sarah Maisey, Patricia Smithen, Anna Vilaro Soler and Tim J. Smith, 'Recovering from Destruction: The Conservation, Reintegration and Perceptual Analysis of a Flood-Damaged Painting by John Martin', in *ICOM-CC 16th Triennial Meeting Lisbon Preprints*, ed. by Janet Bridgland (Paris: International Council of Museums, 2011), paper 682.
35. W. (Bill) Wei, Kate Kornder and Ella Hendriks, *Unpublished Research* (Cultural Heritage Agency of the Netherlands, 2016).
36. Jazzy de Groot, '"Oude Arlésienne" (1988): van esthetisch object naar waarde fragment' (English: "Old Woman from Arles" (1988): From Aesthetic Object to Valuable Fragment) (master's thesis in Dutch, University of Amsterdam, 2015).
37. Davide Massaro, Federica Savazzi, Cinzia Di Dio, David Freedberg, Vittorio Gallese, Gabriella Gilli and Antonella Marchetti, 'When Art Moves the Eyes: A Behavioral and Eye-Tracking Study', *PLoS One*, 7.5 (2012). <https://doi.org/10.1371/journal.pone.0037285>

3 Color

Color unquestionably has and continues to play an important role in the visual arts, design, and media. These roles range from simple decorative roles to more complex roles as a visual language of, among others, emotion, politics and power, social standing, symbolism, and value. The choice of colors which artists use is one of the ways they express these and other messages. How these choices were made have been one of the important subjects of the vast art historical literature.

Most physical, as opposed to digital, works of art fade or discolor with time. As time passes, determining artist intent based on the original colors which were used becomes increasingly difficult. Innovations in the field of so-called color science have provided the art conservation field with important tools to help document works of art in "true" color, but supposedly also to provide a basis for bringing objects back to their original color. In this chapter, innovations in color science are examined which claim to provide the art world with true color documentation and reproduction tools, and supposedly bring heritage professionals closer to what an object originally looked like in terms of color. We then juxtapose this objective technical discussion on color with some brief thoughts on color perception, the question of how people talk about color, and the philosophical question of what color actually is.

3.1 Color science

Since Isaac Newton's well-known experiment, where he showed that white light could be split into many colors using a prism, and then, using another prism, be recombined into white light, scientists have been studying what the nature of light is and how it is perceived. In particular, much research has been conducted on how humans or, more generally, animals see color, how to precisely describe colors, and how to reproduce the color of objects in the best way possible, so-called high-quality reproduction.

A physicist or, more specifically in the case of this book, a color scientist will explain that what humans, and animals in general, see in terms of color is the result of the interaction of visible light rays with an object and how the

DOI: 10.4324/9781003217800-3

light which is reflected from the surface of the object is sensed by the eye. James Maxwell showed that light is a form of electromagnetic radiation. It is now known that visible light is a combination of radiation with a wave form. The wavelengths of this light, between approximately 400 and 700 nanometers (nm), where a nanometer is one-millionth of a millimeter, correspond to particular colors, which humans name as shown schematically in Fig. 3.1. If light with all of those wavelengths shines on an object and the object reflects all of those wavelengths, one sees what is known in the English language as a "white" object. If the object has the property that it can absorb all of the wavelengths, one sees what is known as a "black" object. If the object absorbs some of the wavelengths and reflects the others, one sees something which one calls a particular "color" in the English language.

The amount of each wavelength of light which an object reflects can be measured with a spectrophotometer. The result of such a measurement is a graph known as a reflectance spectrum (see Fig. 3.2). The percentage reflectance (vertical axis) is plotted for each wavelength of visible light (horizontal axis). Four examples of reflectance spectra are shown in Fig. 3.2. For "white," all wavelengths are reflected 100% (Fig. 3.2a), and for a given color, one sees various wavelengths reflected at different percentages (Figs. 3.2bcd). It is important to note that the terms "blue," "red," and "green" are placed in quotation marks in this text on purpose for two reasons, which will be discussed later. The first reason is that there are no natural colors of one single wavelength in nature, that is, one cannot pick out a single wavelength (in Fig. 3.1) and expect to see a color. (Lasers are examples of light with one single wavelength, but those are man-made.) All natural colors will have a distribution of wavelengths with one or two peaks at certain wavelengths. The second reason is that what one person sees and calls "blue," "red," or "green" most likely will not be exactly what someone else sees or calls "blue," "red," or "green."

Fig. 3.1 Schematic diagram showing the wavelengths of visible light, a number of English language designations of the colors an average human would see.

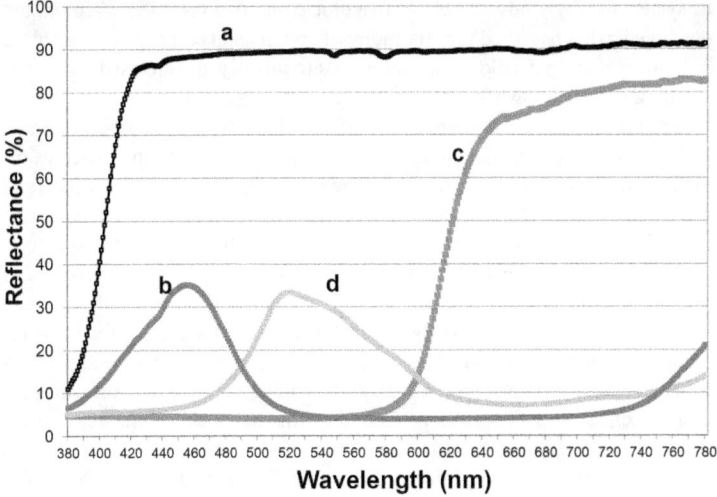

Fig. 3.2 Reflectance spectra measured by a spectrophotometer for something that is
a) "white"
b) "blue"
c) "red"
d) "green"

The way the human eye "sees" is well described in many academic and popular references on vision (see, e.g., [1–4]). The retina is the "sensor" at the back of the eyeball with cells known as rods and cones. The cones are those that are mostly responsible for human color perception in daylight, while the rods are responsible for night vision but do not discern color. Many readers are probably aware that there are three types of cones, sensitive to wavelengths around the colors known in the English language as red, green, or blue (RGB). According to color scientists, what one sees is the information received by the human sensor, the eye, which sends the spectral signals through the optic nerve to the brain, which then processes them so that we see such and such a color (see, e.g., [1–5]).

What this "processing" is, that is, how humans see and perceive color or the world in general, continues to be a major topic of debate between, among others, physicists, physiologists, neurologists, psychologists, and philosophers, as will be discussed in the following sections. On the color science side, this began with empirical research leading to various types of color wheels and charts by, for example, Newton, Goethe, Chevreul, Hering, and Munsell (see, e.g., [6, 7]). Note that the color system developed by Albert Munsell is still used. Michel E. Chevreul was one of the first technologists to systematically study the effect of color combinations on how colors are perceived, what he called the "harmony of colours and contrast" [8]. Many of his concepts underly color design concepts to this day and are used for understanding how artists work with and depict light (e.g., [9]).

Jumping ahead to modern times, color scientists and technologists now understand the concepts of additive and subtractive color mixing, where, simply put, additive mixing occurs when one mixes lights of different colors, and subtractive mixing is what one does when mixing paints of different colors. In terms of the spectra shown in Fig. 3.2, when mixing light, one adds the spectra for different colors together. When mixing paint, one subtracts the spectra of the mixed paints from each other.

In particular, additive mixing of red, green, and blue light is the basis for color television, color computer, and exhibition screens. One finds various RGB models for color used in well-known image-processing software programs such as Adobe Photoshop™. On the other hand, the subtractive CMYK (cyan, yellow, magenta, black) color mixing model is used in the digital printing industry, where closely placed dots of the four colors produce particular colors when viewed from a distance.

While these models are useful for producing something close to what humans see in real life, they do not predict what the human eye sees. One of the most important models for doing this was developed by Kubelka and Munk in the first half of the 20th century [10–12]. It predicts the color of a surface based on the light absorption properties of the surface and the scattering of light due to the surface roughness and index of refraction. The other important development was the CIELAB model for predicting the perception of color. The most recent version (1976) describes colors in three-dimensional graphs in terms of three parameters, lightness (L*) and two factors (a* and b*). The L*a*b* system of designating colors is based on the fact that the brain does not actually process the red, green, and blue spectra it receives directly, but processes differences (opponent color model), in particular, between red and green signals (a*), and blue and yellow signals (b*) [13]. Each combination of value L*, a*, and b* designates a color in this color space. Changes in color, ΔE_{76}, for example, due to the aging of a paint, can be calculated as the square root of $\Delta L^{*2} + \Delta a^{*2} + \Delta b^{*2}$, where the symbol Δ means change, for example, ΔL^* is L* of the new paint minus L* of the aged paint. Color perception testing is often conducted using the CIELAB color space and is based on the results of human subjects being asked to look at colors which they see through an aperture with an opening of 2 degrees. Color matches or differences are determined as the average of the results of several test subjects. The resulting L*a*b* color is said to be what an average test subject sees, the so-called standard colorimetric observer, the CIE 2° observer.

With this understanding of light reflection/absorption and of how humans perceive color, color scientists can now help conservators and other museum professionals understand how lighting affects how a work of art appears. For example, L*a*b* colors can be associated with spectral reflection measurements. Using those relationships, the concept of metamerism can be explained, the phenomenon where two colors with different reflectance spectra can appear the same to the human eye under one set of lighting conditions, but different under another set of lighting conditions. Color scientists claim that the models also allow them to calculate how a painting may originally have looked based on paint recipes which have been determined chemically (see Section 1.3), or after a varnish is removed (see, e.g., [5, 14]).

The development of digital imaging systems based on CCD and CMOS sensor technologies along with color science theory led to the development of the first digital cameras which could be used to produce color images [15, 16]. Early color digital cameras and many current consumer models used red, green, and blue filters to produce three images. These raw images could then be further processed in imaging computer software written by the developers, eventually leading to commercially available programs such as the well-known Adobe Photoshop™ program, which mathematically transforms the raw image into an RGB color image.

These innovations in digital imaging combined with the color theory just discussed have taken art conservation and documentation even further, resulting in the capability for documenting and reproducing works of art in "true color." Digital imaging has the advantage that the colors do not fade, although one disadvantage is that because advances in hardware technology continue to be so rapid, making sure the images remain accessible and readable is a major problem.

In the cultural heritage world, the Doerner Institut (Munich, Germany) and the National Gallery in London carried out some of the first studies during the 1990s, using the innovative digital imaging techniques in order to produce true color images of works of art with high pixel resolution. This work included the VASARI (Visual Arts System for Archiving and Retrieval of Images 1989–1992) [17–19] and MARC (Methodology for Art Reproduction in Color 1995–1998) [20] projects. These projects, funded by the European Union research organization (ESPRIT II and III programs), were the first steps in research which is still continuing, allowing museums to digitize and reproduce works of art in high color resolution so that people around the world can see them in virtual museums and other sources on the internet.

This early research focused on two-dimensional objects, essentially paintings. Entire paintings could not be photographed at high spatial resolution at once. Using precision motorized stages, digital images could be taken sequentially, horizontally, and vertically, row by row, column by column. The resulting images were then "stitched" together by matching the boundaries of neighboring images to create a complete color image of a painting.

Since then, digital camera technology has advanced in leaps and bounds with the development of high-resolution CCD and CMOS sensor chips in combination with red, green, and blue filters (see [21, 22] for a brief review of digital imaging equipment). For high-resolution digital photography of nonmoving objects such as most works of art, the sensors can be scanned within the digital cameras and images taken for each of the three colored filters. The sensors can be moved to take multiple shots behind each of the filters mounted in various arrays of red, green, and blue, resulting in higher color resolution. An example is the "four-shot" mode where the sensor takes an image behind each of the red and blue filters, and two behind the green filter, simulating the ratio of red, blue, and green cone cells in the human eye. The red, green, and blue filters can also be permanently mounted on the sensor so that a color image is taken in "one shot." Though it takes time, up to minutes to image a work of art, and longer for the proper processing of the raw image to the colored result, such techniques have resulted in high-quality color images.

Large improvements in resolution have since been developed within the art conservation world based on commercially available digital sensors using the concept of the filter wheel. Instead of using red, green, and blue filters, which is essentially the measurement of the reflectance spectrum of each pixel of the object in broad bands of the visible spectrum, color scientists now make use of wavelength filters covering much smaller ranges of the spectrum. For each pixel of a painting, they can obtain a more complete color spectrum using several filters, so-called multi-spectral imaging. By using filters which are now available and which cover down to only ten nanometers of the visible light region, one can almost image a continuous spectrum for each pixel of a painting. This use of many such narrow filters to obtain an image is known as hyperspectral imaging [23–26]. When using ten nanometer filters for example, one obtains 30 spectral images for every pixel of a painting.

One can use the individual images, for example, to determine if a particular pigment is present in a particular pixel of the image. The pigment will only show up in the images of the wavelength filters corresponding to the color of the pigment. One can then produce maps of particular pigments by only showing the images for those specific wavelengths. At the other end of the scale from a full-sized camera, fiber optics allows identifying pigments at a very local scale ([e.g., 27]). This use of digital imaging has developed into a much-needed tool for nondestructive methods for identifying pigments in paintings, rather than the destructive (taking a specimen) and complex chemical analyses techniques discussed in Section 1.3.

By combining all of the 30 partial spectra into one, one can calculate the total reflectance spectrum of the pixel in L*a*b* (CIELAB) units. With this information, one can convert the data to RGB or CMYK values and obtain a high-resolution color image of the painting for the computer screen or print media. This is what color scientists call a "true color" image.

The color scientist, Roy Berns, summarizes this all as follows:

The goal of spectral color reproduction is to match the spectral reflectance properties of the artwork. This requires a multi- or hyperspectral camera and a printing system whose ink and paper can match the artwork's spectral properties. Spectral color reproduction has two advantages. First, the reproduction matches the original under any lighting condition and when viewed by any observer. The print will match the painting both in the imaging studio and in the gallery. Second, the painting and the print will have the same color inconstancy. By taking the print outdoors, we can see how the painting appeared to a *plein air* artist. The spectral match is also a colorimetric match, with CIELAB coordinates for both the painting and the print that are identical for all observers and all lighting conditions.

[28]

Color science has also led to other innovative uses of digital techniques. In particular, techniques such as virtual retouching and rendering will be discussed in Chapter 5. Art conservation and art history have certainly benefited from this nondestructive manner for studying pigments in (polychrome) works of art. However, the reader will have noted that many of the color terms used in this section have appeared in quotation marks, including the word color itself. The assumption behind all of the work in color science and the application of the results is that what is measured can be correctly and precisely translated into color which people see. The next two sections will take a critical look at this assumption.

3.2 Color is language

Terwijl ik luisterde kwam de zon op. Ik zou de werkelijkheid geweld aandoen door haar opgang te beschrijven als rozevingerig, maar er was roze te zien, en geel, en verder weg wat paarsblauw aan de onderzijde van een lage wolkenbank, en oker, en bleekgroen, en nog een paar kleuren die zich niet gemakkelijk laten in taal laten vangen, die je liever in handen zou geven van een schilder, die je graag zou willen terugzien op een groot doek, op een heel kalme manier aangebracht, maar die iedereen die ze ziet hoe dan ook in vervoering brengt.

Sander Kollaard, "De Kleuren van Anna"
(English: "Anna's Colors") [29]

While I was listening, the sun rose. I would really do a disservice to the sunrise by describing it as being like pinkish fingers, but one could see pink, and yellow, and a little farther away a bit of purplish blue under the low bank of clouds, and ochre, and pale green, and a few other colors which are not easy to put into language, which you would rather put in the hands of a painter, and that you would gladly be able to see again on a large canvas, applied in a calm manner, but where everyone who saw it would be enraptured by it.

(Translation: W. (Bill) Wei)

The author Sander Kollaard wishes that a painter could be with him to paint the colors of sunrise which he cannot put into language. Then he can continue to be enraptured by what he saw on that one morning, without having to have to try to figure out how to describe it. However, as was seen in the previous section, color scientists have come a long way in developing a reference code or language for colors based on the CIE 2° observer. In that way, they help art historians, conservators, and other viewers of art understand the colors they see and what effects they have on each other. They supposedly can also say specifically which colors a work of art has, and calculate the exact pink or yellow or purplish blue which Kollaard would like to have the painter reproduce. What one sees is the information received by the human sensor, the eye, which sends the spectral signals to the brain, which then processes them so that we see such and such a color (see, e.g., [1, 3, 5, 30]). Or so the color scientists claim and so would many cultural heritage professionals like to think.

But there are two major weaknesses to the argument that color science and the associated innovative technology can help us fully understand color, its relationships, and its changes in works of art. The first weakness is the problem which Kollaard has, that is, how to describe the various colors which he sees to others, in the assumption that they will also understand and see what he sees. It goes without saying that he is not going to write his description in L*a*b* notation. This will be discussed in the following paragraphs. The second weakness is a result of posing a more fundamental question, and that is, what is color and what is it that the brain is actually processing. This second weakness of color science will be discussed in the following section.

Reflectance spectra which color scientists measure may be considered objective. Top-of-the-line digital imaging systems now available can measure up to millions of different colors. The question that Kollaard raises is, however, "what do I call all of those colors?" In virtually all color science research in art conservation which is written in the English language, it is tacitly accepted that spectral reflectance spectra with peaks at the lower values of visible wavelengths near 400 nm are called some form of blue, reflectance spectra at the high wavelengths around 700 nm are some form of red, and combinations of peaks at different wavelengths, are, for example, some degree of green or yellow, as seen in Fig. 3.1. The reader can see immediately that there is nothing objective about giving a name to particular spectrum. In a university lecture on perception given to beginning conservation students, the author compliments one of the students on her green blouse, to the consternation of all of those present who think that they see an orange blouse with a tint of red. To take the thought further, for all intents and purposes one can call the spectra near 400 nm chartreuse, and the spectra near 700 nm globuflan [*sic*]. In fact, color naming in the cultural heritage profession largely makes use of Western terminology.

That color is a cultural and language construct is also obvious in the art historical literature, which is rife with debates over the definitions and translations of color names from different languages, and nuances used by artists and their contemporaries. Artists do not work with spectral measurements nor can one always assume that what they mixed is as uniform as what a color scientist is trying to reproduce in the laboratory, either by following old recipes or performing digital color modeling. The question is thus if "objective" color scientists can characterize, model, and predict color usage as accurately as they claim.

Looking a little closer at color language, one notes that colors have always held an important place in history, and certain colors such as blue or violet, as well as the precious metals, were considered to be more valuable than others because they were all hard to come by (see, e.g., [31, 32]). One can consider Isaac Newton's experiment of producing the rainbow of colors from white light through a prism as the beginning of a system for the naming of colors. More than one author has noted that he chose to name seven colors, red, orange, yellow, green, blue, indigo and violet, which coincide with the number of tones in a Western music scale [e.g., Wasserman cited in 33]. With these two examples, one already sees the subjectivity of color naming and interpretation. Besides the historically important color wheels and charts mentioned previously, artists (including Munsell) themselves have been active in trying to understand and name colors, for example, Josef Albers, Johannes Itten, and the pointillists George Seurat and Paul Signac [34–36].

In fact, many color design experts, linguists, and anthropologists have shown that color names are not reflectance spectra, but a product of a culture and its language (see, e.g., [37–40]). Duckworth and Sassin note in the introduction to their book on ancient and medieval art:

One difficulty is that linguistic categorization introduces a certain amount of bias to studies of these phenomena, particularly when an attempt is made to unify the study of color and light across cultures. Because we can only express our individual color experience through language, the latter has been central to the psychology and anthropology of color, but language is itself inherently subjective and open to multiple interpretations.

[41]

Pastoureau writes, as cited by Van Leeuwen, "Color is defined first of all as a social phenomenon. It is the society that 'makes' the color, that gives it its definitions and meanings, that constructs its codes and ethics, that organizes its customs and determines its stakes" [42]. Van Leeuwen writes further, "There is no transcultural truth to color perception" [43]. He also notes that

> Hugo Magnus, a German ophthalmologist, conducted ethnographic research among the Ovahero in South-West Africa, to prove that colour naming and color perception are two different things, and that primitive people see color in exactly the same way as 'civilized' people. These early writings set the science for a debate on color naming that continues today and is still dominated by the same issues – the difference between color naming and color perception which was first studied by Magnus, and the different ways in which colors are classified in different contexts.
>
> [44]

Berlin and Kay proposed that different cultures have a different number of basic color terms [45]. More so-called advanced civilizations have 11 basic colors in their vocabulary, while more so-called primitive cultures have fewer. Although they were one of the first to theorize that there are cultural differences in color names, their work has since been criticized for being too strongly based on the Western Munsell color naming system (e.g., [46]). In particular, Wierzbicka clearly shows that color language is strongly culture-dependent, and that there are cultures which do not have color words (or even a word for "color") but use terms from nature to indicate, for example, different shades of green or blue [47]. Further, it is noted that many cultures such as those in Indonesia do not have words for colors when presented with color charts for testing [48] or do not really talk about color [49].

Latour has noted the complexity of using standardization, again the Munsell system, to solve the problem of language. He observed scientists studying Amazon soils, and how they determined the color of the soil by "sticking clods of Earth in Munsell charts" [50]. This gave them a number which they could use to describe the color of the soil, not trusting their own memory or language to remember the color. Latour also notes how the same scientists struggled to characterize the soils by describing their taste.

However, this raises the question of how such a limited vocabulary can be used to describe the millions of colors which a digital imaging professional can measure. John Gage already posed this question in the early 1990s:

> For the student of languages the chief problem has been to account for the fact that although the human eye is capable of discriminating some millions of color nuances, most color-languages, in all cultures and throughout recorded history, include a vocabulary of from eight to eleven 'basic' terms. . . . Color-salience as revealed by language must be related to the wider experience of color in a given culture, this experience differing among the different groups within this culture to whom color is of some

concern. . . . And yet, of course, color-space has never been more than partially and crudely mapped by color-language.

[51]

"It is also clear that for many people, unless they are professionally engaged in color-technology, this reduced color-vocabulary has a powerful effect on perception itself. So color-perception and color-language turn out to be closely bound up with each other" [52]. Koenderink agrees with this line of thinking:

> The systems currently in common use (mainly the Munsell system and the CIE Lab system) are feeble, ad hoc constructions based upon uneasy combinations of colorimetry (the objective ingredient) and 'psychophysical data', that is to say arbitrary selection and functional fits decreed by a committee.
>
> [53]

M. Tye also questions whether humans or animals use the color discrimination capabilities they have. "Long ago, Mother Nature equipped humans and many other creatures with a color detection system because it was adaptive. Creatures with color vision were better able to identify things that were good to eat via their colors than creatures without it. . . . But grass does not look *exactly* the same shade of green in all these conditions. . . . So, she decided to formulate instructions for equipping the descendants of these creatures with a system for reliably detecting the *coarse-grained* colors of things. Her overriding concern was that the system be such that, when operating as designed with respect to the detection of coarse-grained colors in the right kind of environment, it enable its users to be as successful as the most successful of their ancestors" [54]. And further:

> The truth about true blue and other determinate hues at its level of grain is that Mother Nature did not bother to design us so as to detect *them*. There was no point in Her doing so. No selectional advantage would have accrued. Thus, even when everything is working as it should, still sometimes a surface can look true blue and not be. This did not worry Mother Nature; and it should not worry us either.
>
> [55]

One only has to look at the difficulty in translating English color terms into some other European language to see the difficulty of such a limited vocabulary. Even in Western cultures, translating a color word into another language is a difficult and subjective exercise. This author, having lived in the United States, Germany, and The Netherlands, has noted, for example, that what is called orange in the United States is more likely to be called red, "rot" or "rood," in Germany and The Netherlands, respectively. Gage notes further over the debate on color language, "Several themes return repeatedly, such as the feeling that verbal language is incapable of defining the experience of color" [56].

Even artists know that selecting color is a combination of cultural and personal perspectives. The Copenhagen artist Tal R notes:

> I think a painter can't have failed colors. Also even the best painters are not necessarily experts in colors. They are expert in putting ideas through colors and speaking with ideas in colors. People are expert in mixing or looking at colors one by one. That's something else." And further, "I think it's all about experience. Narratives are different in different cultures and Trieste [*author: a color he developed for Fritz Hansen*] is for me something which is very different from you.

[57]

A further complication is the difference in ways of seeing and perceiving color within a single culture. It has long been known that individuals who look at the same object in context do not see exactly the same color. It has been shown that men and women do not see a particular color in the same way [58]. The way children see colors changes with age, not only as a result of learning but also changes in the visual system itself [59]. Color scientists tell us that the CIE standard observer sees the visible light spectrum in such and such a manner. The CIE observer concept has in fact shown its value for testing and standardization using a color reference state, the CIELAB model discussed in the previous section, for the production and quality control of colored consumer products, paints, color printing, and so forth. However, as Thompson points out [60], individual humans are not the standard observer. Having subjects conduct a CIE observer experiment comparing colors through an aperture is not the same as observing a solid object. This difference in viewing so-called surface and film colors as would be seen in a CIE test was already noted by Katz in the first half of the 20th century [61] and discussed in [62].

To further confuse the issue, one must also consider the not insignificant number of people with various versions of color blindness, and the less commonly known condition known as synesthesia, a condition in certain individuals where a stimulant for one of the five senses triggers a response in one or more of the other senses [63, 64]. The most well-known form of color-blindness is that in which a person does not see red or green due to a congenital disorder or disease affecting the cones in the retina [65]. Research is being conducted to help color-blind people recover original color, whatever that may be. But even then, the efficacy of solutions can only be determined by subjective testing with human subjects. Turning that around, it is noted by Bernárdez-Vilaboa that, "Any subjective evaluation procedure for a work of art can be affected by lighting and the living eye" [66]. People with synesthesia report that rather than just seeing colors, they also hear them, for example, a boy hears a frog croaking when he sees the color blue [67], or they may see or experience color when they see letters or numbers [68].

If one considers art conservation, the issue of the necessity for color precision can be also asked in relation to one of the issues faced by museum and collection managers, that is, how often one is allowed to exhibit objects which are sensitive to light. Brokerhof has performed perception studies on color changes [69], asking subjects how they would value various stages of the fading of historical maps. Brokerhof uses the so-called unit of "just noticeable color change" (jnc) which is a ΔE_{76} value of 1.5. This value is nowhere as precise as one of those 64 million digital color differences. The chance that someone will remember a pixel difference is also quite negligible [70].

Many conservators will argue, with the codes of ethics on being informed in mind, that every pixel change is important. However, one is talking about preserving works of art for generations, if not centuries. On the one hand, it might be academically interesting to know at what pixel rate colors change in order to predict how long they may be exhibited under a certain intensity of light. On the other hand, given the current weak state of predictive modeling for aging and the amount of scatter in the data, one wonders why one needs pixel precision for something that is only visible at a ΔE color change level after many years. It may also be asked how important the works of art that are now being studied in such color detail will even be so many years later, an issue which will be discussed further in Chapter 6.

The questionability of the use of high-precision color measurements also comes into play when considering the physical retouching of a painting or polychrome object. Conservators are tasked with producing a color which either matches and/or blends in with the color surrounding the area which is to be retouched, or when filling in a lacune with a neutral color, selecting a color that does not detract from its surroundings. They must ultimately mix the paints as called for in a recipe found in the literature or developed by the color scientist or chemist. If information is lacking, they must try to find a mixture that matches what is on the painting. The conservator must also try to match the brushstrokes of the artist, an issue which will be discussed in more detail in the next chapter. Retouching is therefore a task requiring expertise and hand skills which only a trained conservator has. The objectivity of recipes provides a paint mixture which may be close to the original, but which actual paint mixture will be used at a particular point on the painting is still ultimately the subjective decision of the conservator. It will also be shown in Section 3.4 that even though the color may be "correct," the texture will often make a retouch visible on a monochrome painting.

One must then consider that the "untrained" lay viewer is even less exacting. A simple experiment which the author conducted at a science fair in The Netherlands for children and their parents showed these differences in perception. A photocopy print was made of a red patch of a Mondriaan painting with a hole made in it. The RGB value of the red patch was determined using Photoshop™. Children (and their parents) were asked to match five prints of reds made with the same photocopier with slightly different RGB values as the Mondriaan. It was noted that children made their decisions very quickly, and those decisions were spread evenly among the five different reds. The (fewer) parents took much longer to make their decisions, and only chose three of the reds. This difference between children and adults, and within each group, is similar to that found with the more sophisticated eye-tracking test discussed in Section 2.3.

The point of this section can be summarized in the following two quotes from Van Leeuwen:

> There has never been a single language of color. Color codes with a restricted semantic reach have always proliferated and sometimes contradicted each other. For some centuries now, there has been a mismatch between a color theory based on physical facts and a color theory based on psychological effects. The two theories, the scientific theory of color form and the psychological theory of color meaning, do not easily fit and theorists and artists alike have struggled with this problem.

[71]

And further, "Color measurement is important for companies that develop and market colors and colorful objects. . . . But colorimetric systems have not replaced color names." And "looking a little further than the color wheels of the textbooks, we can see that 'Western' color names are not all that different from those of other cultures. They are just as motivated by interest as the systems of traditional cultures. It is just that the 'things of extraordinary interest' and the 'things that dominate people's view' in everyday urban life are rather different" [72].

3.3   The philosophy of color

In the previous section, the schism between objective high-resolution color measurements and the language of color was discussed. Van Leeuwen notes in the history of color since Newton, that

> color was now split into two disciplines that did not sit easily with each other – on the one hand chemistry and physics, and later the physiology of color perception, sciences which looked at color as an objective phenomenon, separate from the subjective, human world; on the other hand, the emerging psychology of color, which gave a central place to human subjectivity.

[73]

This now brings up a philosophical question which can be illustrated by a riddle which this author first heard in grade school and does not know where it came from, "If there is lightning on an uninhabited island, is there thunder?" One can pose a similar question as follows, "If there is an object on an uninhabited island, does it have color?"

The perception of color and perception in general are far from being understood. The following discussion is not meant to be read as a review of the literature on this subject, but as an indication of the problems being faced by perception scientists. There are a number of theories for how human perception works. These are grouped into roughly two types (see, e.g., [74]). One type includes the so-called constructivist theories where the brain receives sensory information, and neural processes interpret that information. The other group include so-called direct theories where the visual system gathers information based on what J.J. Gibson referred to as affordances, "a bundle of properties which gives us the opportunity to perceive something specific or to move through the world" [75], or, more generally, they are properties of an object that "are to be understood as possibilities for *action* provided to an animal by the environment" [76].

As discussed in Section 3.1, color scientists assume that objects are colored and that the human visual system is designed to sense these colors and somehow interpret them, that is, they work implicitly from the constructivist approach. The retina obtains information from incoming light, and this is sent to the brain. There, the neural systems process the information, and we therefore see color, for example, using the three-dimensional space described in Section 3.1. The color scientist, Roy Berns, writes:

> Today we know that color occurs in the brain; it is the endpoint of a sequence of physical, physiological, and psychological events. But color is, in a sense, in the world as well: objects have color. . . . Although it may seem paradoxical to state that color occurs in the brain, then, this is readily validated by our ability to produce the identical color sensation using many different combinations of colorants and coloring techniques. Color displays reproduce our chromatic world, composed of hundreds of colorants, with only three colored lights. Most printing systems use only four inks. If color were exclusively a physical property, materials would match only when their positions were identical, thus producing identical spectral signatures.
>
> [77]

The question is if there is indeed a paradox as Berns writes. As Faber Birren puts it, "Perception struggles to see the world as normal under astonishingly varied conditions of illumination" [78]. There is a large literature on the philosophy of color and color perception. In an extensive review by Thompson [79], past and current theories are discussed. There is the objective view about color which states that an object has some physical property which produces a color which the viewer sees. This is the basis of computational modeling performed by color scientists, where the external object/world is sensed by the retina, and this information must somehow be processed to provide an internal representation. Then, there is the subjective view about color, which says that an object is not in itself colored, but has the disposition (or using Gibson's term, affordance) to appear that way to a viewer under certain circumstances. Thompson also speaks of a theory that "colours are entirely in the head; they are nothing but sensations of a certain type. Colours are projected on to the world, but there no further sense in which the world is coloured" [80]. Baxandall notes:

> [C]olor is an accident of vision, a function of the beholder not an intrinsic quality of real objects, whereas form is not only real but offers the security of perception through more than one sense, since we can apprehend form not only with vision but also with touch.
>
> [81]

There are also theories which consider color perception to be relational in nature, thus lying somewhere between the various other theories. Quoting Cohen [82], "colors are not (as the physicalist maintains) subject- and condition-independent properties of their bearers, but relational properties constituted in terms of relations to subjects and viewing conditions." Thompson takes this a step further in his ecological view that perception is a result of the relationship between objects and the animal/human moving through the environment.

Given the difficulty humans have in studying and understanding their own perception, the paradox that Berns has may be a result of the computational manner of understanding color perception. The computational models used by color scientists cannot account for all colors which can be perceived, which indicates that there is more to color perception than color science can account for using a standard observer [83].

Another problem for color scientists trying to precisely calculate what it is that a human sees in terms of color is the concept of color constancy (see, e.g., [62, 84–86]). Color constancy is the term for the fact that humans see a color no matter what the lighting and surroundings are. Birren notes:

> This may be confusing (or perhaps academic), for the human sense of illumination is so automatic and natural as to make a person more or less unconscious of it. Perhaps it seldom, if ever, occurs to painters that their works continually look the same, morning, noon and night (under artificial light), in their studios, in a museum or gallery, up on a roof or down in a cellar. This magic is obviously not in the eye it is in the brain, in perception.
>
> [87]

Birren provides a good example of color constancy, comparing a human observation with a photograph of the same situation:

A gray hen standing in full sunlight in a barnyard and a white hen standing in the shade of the barn would appear gray and white respectively if you witnessed the scene, even though the gray hen reflected more light into your eye that did the white hen. A camera in this instance would record literally all light energy that struck the film. In any such photograph the small patch of the gray hen that stood in sunlight might look white while the small patch of the white hen that stood in shadow might look gray.

[88]

Mausfeld [89] points out, that the dependence on "common sense" and on the use of computations to predict color appearance is one of the critical weaknesses in trying to determine what color is, and more generally in what perception is. It assumes that the calculation in the brain produces a result that is what the object has as a property. The sensory system of humans, or animals general may detect certain wavelengths. But the traditional assumption is that there is some kind of computational process going on in the brain which results in a specific answer. It seems to work. However, there is enough evidence of the variation in how humans view a specific color they may call 'green', to show that this assumption does not hold. And the question of how non-humans perceive color has been left out of this discussion.

What Mausfeld implies is that color scientists use instruments to sense color and then use the same instruments to calculate which (CIELAB) colors the instruments see. And because these are supposed to be "true colors," the art and art conservation use them as the objective basis for their research and conservation decisions. But Mausfeld writes about research on perception in general:

At the roots of these intuitions is our conviction that perception basically works the way it appears to us. It is, however, an essential part of the functioning of our brain that it does not provide us with mechanisms to observe its own machinery, and this also holds for what may be distinguished as the perceptual system.

(90, see also his discussion in 91)

He and a number of other color experts and philosophers seriously question the assumption that there is "color, per se," Already early in the development of color science, the research scientist Joseph Sheppard warned about misusing CIELAB standards for judging appearance,

it seems unrealistic to expect people not to associate some concept of expected 'appearance' with a given CIE specification and it is to such an expected appearance that the 'response' of the CIE Standard Observer refers herein. While thus recognizing the usefulness of the concept, the reader must be cautioned that it is fraught with danger. when a particular color doesn't have the 'expected' appearance, the CIE System must not be blamed. CIE specifications . . . say nothing about appearance.

[92]

Up to this point, the discussion has concerned what color one sees from an external object. There is, however, the question as to how humans see color even if there is no external stimulation. Birren and Westphal mention internal color phenomena such as colors produced by putting pressure on the eyeballs, and colors induced by hallucinogens and after images [93, 94]. Already in 1976 Birren notes, "What is clearly appreciated today is that the experience of color has an amazing degree of independence of external physical facts" [87].

Given this discussion on the philosophy of color, the question is as follows: what does innovative color science really do for art conservation?

3.4   Retouching monochrome paintings

In order to start the discussion about the question just posed at the end of the previous section, a case study led by this author involving the retouching of a monochrome painting is presented [95]. Conservators had made a number of attempts over several years trying to retouch scratches on a monochrome painting, *Blauwe Tafel* (Blue Table, 1977), by the Dutch artist, Jan Roeland. They tried various paint mixtures to try to match the color on the canvas, but the retouching was always visible. Because this was not successful, the Cultural Heritage Agency of the Netherlands was asked to analyze the paints. This was done, and possible recipes were developed based on a cross-section chemical analysis of the ratios of pigment types found, and spectrophotometric measurements taken at locations near the scratches. The conservator was asked to systematically follow the recipes and to first make several samples for spectrophotometric analysis and comparison with the spectra from the painting. Based on this, the proper paint mixture was supposed to be selected. However, in spite of the possibilities for spectral matching, the conservator, as they are often wont to do, decided to go the practical route and eye-balled the final color. The final recipe was unfortunately not documented, but spectral analysis did show an excellent match. However, upon retouching, the retouch could still be easily seen as it was in the earlier unsuccessful attempts. It was found that this was because the conservator carefully dotted paint onto the scratches as prescribed by traditional techniques based on conservation ethics. However, the technique did not at all match the paintbrush strokes of the undamaged surroundings. This produced a different micro-texture than the rest of the painting, and thus a micro-shadowing effect which made the retouches visible.

This case study shows the strength of many technical advances in chemistry and color science, the ability to determine paint composition and calculate possible paint recipes, and to produce paint mixtures which can be matched with the painting using high-resolution spectrophotometric techniques. However, it also showed, though unintentionally, that the trained conservator's eye may still be required to find the ultimate match. More importantly, it showed that color is hardly the only property of an object that determines its appearance. Texture also plays an important role in the conservation of paintings and polychrome objects.

3.5   Summary of Chapter 3

In this chapter, innovation and developments in the field of color science in art conservation over the past few decades were examined and placed in the context of the science of color perception and the philosophy of what color even is. In a sense, one could conclude that the term "color science" is a misnomer. The following points were discussed. A brief history of color science begins with Isaac Newton's experiment with the breaking of white light into color using a prism, and culminates in the development of standard CIELAB color models which provide a reference standard for calculating and designating colors based on reflectance spectra. The combination of these models with advances in digital imaging now provides the art and art conservation world with high-resolution tools for documenting and reproducing works of art in millions of "true colors," as well as a nondestructive tool for identifying pigments and how artists used them.

Color is, however, language and not digital data. Given the limited capabilities of languages to name and describe colors consistently, and the complexities of human (color) perception, it is questioned what it is that color science and digital imaging innovations are providing. The answer to this question becomes all the more complex given that philosophers and perception scientists still cannot define what color is, or, for that matter, any of the other four human senses. However, the human eye can still see that a "true color" reproduction of a work of art still doesn't look quite real because the reproduction cannot provide the sense of roughness or texture of the surface of a work. A case study on the retouching of monochrome paintings demonstrates that the human eye, which is less capable of distinguishing colors than digital technology, is still required to match colors.

References

1. Joseph J. Sheppard, Jr., *Human Color Perception – A Critical Study of the Experimental Foundation* (New York: American Elsevier Publishing Corporation, 1968).
2. *The Colour Image Processing Handbook*, ed. by Stephen J. Sangwine and R.E.N. Horne (London: Chapman & Hall, 1998).

3. *La couleur: Lumière, vision et matériaux*, ed. by Mady Elias and Jacques Lafait (Paris: Éditions Belin, 2006).

4. *The Perception of Colour*, ed. by Peter Gouras (London: The Macmillan Press, 1991).

5. Roy S. Berns, *Color Science and the Visual Arts – A Guide for Conservators, Creators and the Curious* (Los Angeles: Getty Conservation Institute, 2016).

6. John Gage, *Color and Culture – Practice and Meaning from Antiquity to Abstraction* (Berkeley: University of California Press, 1993).

7. Harald Küppers, *Schnellkurs Farbenlehre* (Cologne: DuMont Literatur und Kunstverlag, 2005), pp. 31–67.

8. M. E. Chevreul, *The Principles of Harmony and Contrast of Colors and Their Application to the Arts*, based on the first English edition of 1854 translated from the first French edition of 1939 (New York: Reinhold Publishing, 1967), p. 105ff.

9. John S. Werner and Floyd Ratliff, 'Some Origins of the Lightness and Darkness of Colors – In the Visual Art and in the Brain', *Techne*, 9–10 (1999), 61–73.

10. Paul Kubelka and Franz Munk, 'Ein Beitrag zur Optik der Farbanstriche', *Zeitschrift für Technische Physik*, 12 (1931), 593–601.

11. Paul Kubelka, 'New Contributions to the Optics of Intensely Light-Scattering Materials. Part I', *Journal of the Optical Society of America*, 38.5 (1948), 448–457, errata 1067.

12. Paul Kubelka, 'New Contributions to the Optics of Intensely Light-Scattering Materials. Part II', *Journal of the Optical Society of America*, 44.4 (1954), 330–335.

13. Evan Thompson, *Colour Vision – A Study in Cognitive Science and the Philosophy of Perception* (London: Routledge, 1995), pp. 51–65.

14. Mady Elias, Nadejda Mas and Pascal Cotte, 'Review of Several Optical Non-Destructive Analyses of an Easel Painting. Complementarity and Crosschecking of the Results', *Journal of Cultural Heritage*, 12.4 (2011), 335–345.

15. A. Kazlauciunas, 'Digital Imaging – Theory and Application Part I: Theory', *Surface Coatings International Part B: Coatings Transactions*, 84.B1 (2001), 1–19.

16. A. Kazlauciunas, 'Digital Imaging – Theory and Application Part II: Application', *Surface Coatings International Part B: Coatings Transactions*, 84.B2 (2001), 91–168.

17. Martinez Kirk, 'High Resolution Digital Imaging of Paintings: The Vasari Project', *Microcomputers for Information Management*, 8.4 (1991), 277–283.

18. Andreas Burmester, John Cupitt, Hervé Derrien, Nikolaos Dessipris, Anthony Hamber, Kirk Martinez, Manfred Müller and David Saunders, 'The Examination of Paintings by Digital Image Analysis', in *ART '92–3rd International Conference on Non-Destructive Testing, Microanalytical Methods and Environment Evaluation for Study and Conservation of Works of Art*, October 4–8, 1992, Viterbo, ICCROM (Rome: International Centre for the Study of the Preservation and the Restoration of Cultural Property and Milan: Consiglio Nazionale dell Ricerche, 1992), pp. 201–214.

19. David Saunders and John Cupitt, 'Image Processing at the National Gallery: The VASARI Project', *National Gallery Technical Bulletin*, 14 (1993), 72–85.

20. D. Saunders, John Cupitt, Colin White and Sarah Holt, 'The MARC II Camera and the Scanning Initiative at the National Gallery', *National Gallery Technical Bulletin*, 23 (2002), 76–82.

21. Romano Padeste, 'Imaging Systems', in *FOCAL Encyclopedia of Photography*, ed. by Michael R. Peres, 4th edn (Amsterdam: Focal Press, Elsevier, 2007), pp. 364–370.
22. Michael Kriss, 'Solid State Imaging Sensors', in *FOCAL Encyclopedia of Photography*, ed. by Michael R. Peres, 4th edn (Amsterdam: Focal Press, Elsevier, 2007), pp. 370–371.
23. Alejandro Ribes and Ruven Pillay, 'Studying That Smile: A Tutorial on Multispectral Imaging of Paintings Using the Mona Lisa as a Case Study', *IEEE Signal Processing Magazine* (2008). <https://doi.org/10.1109/MSP.2008.923091>
24. John K. Delaney, Kathryn A. Dooley, Annelies van Loon and Abbie Vandivere, 'Mapping the Pigment Distribution of Vermeer's *Girl with a Pearl Earring*', *Heritage Science*, 8.4 (2020). <https://doi.org/10.1186/s40494-019-0348-9>
25. Marcello Picollo, Costanza Cucci, Andrea Casini and Lorenzo Stefani, 'Hyper-Spectral Imaging Technique in the Cultural Heritage Field: New Possible Scenarios', *Sensors*, 20.10 (2020). <https://doi.org/10.3390/s20102843>
26. Silvia A. Centeno, Charlotte Hale, Federico Caró, Anna Cesaratto, Nobuko Shibayama, John Delaney, Kathryn Dooley, Geert van der Snickt, Koen Janssens and Susan Alyson Stein, 'Van Gogh's. *Irises* and *Roses*: The Contribution of Chemical Analysis and Imaging to the Assessment of Color Changes in the Red Lake Pigments', *Heritage Science*, 5.18 (2017). <https://doi.org/10.1186/s40494-017-0131-8>
27. Guillaume Dupuis, Mady Elias and Lionel Simonot, 'Pigment Identification by Fiber-Optics Diffuse Reflectance Spectroscopy', *Applied Spectroscopy*, 56.10 (2002), 1329–1336.
28. Roy S. Berns, 'Color Reproduction', in *Color Science and the Visual Arts – A Guide for Conservators, Creators and the Curious* (Los Angeles: Getty Conservation Institute, 2016), Chapter 7, pp. 183–189.
29. Sander Kollaard, *De Kleuren van Anna* (English title 'Anna's Colors') (Amsterdam: Uitgeverij van Oorschot, 2021), pp. 65–66.
30. Harald Küppers, *Das Grundgesetz der Farbenlehre* (Cologne: DuMont Buchverlag, 1978).
31. John Gage, *Color and Culture – Practice and Meaning from Antiquity to Abstraction* (Berkeley: University of California Press, 1993).
32. John Gage, *Colour and Meaning – Art, Science and Symbolism* (London: Thames & Hudson, 1999).
33. Evan Thompson, *Colour Vision – A Study in Cognitive Science and the Philosophy of Perception* (London: Routledge, 1995), p. 4.
34. Jo Kirby, Kate Stonor, Ashok Roy, Aviva Burnstock, Rachel Grout and Raymond White, 'Seurat's Painting Practice: Theory, Development and Technology', *National Gallery Technical Bulletin*, 24 (2003), 4–37.
35. Josef Albers, *Interaction of Color*, revised and expanded edn (New Haven: Yale University, 1975).
36. Johannes Itten, *Kleurenleer* (De Bilt: Cantecleer, 1970).
37. Ulf Klrén and Karin Fridell Anter, 'Seeing Color', in *Color and Design*, ed. by Marilyn DeLong and Barbara Martinson (London: Berg, 2012), Chapter 1, pp. 3–17.
38. Anna Wierzbicka, 'The Meaning of Color Terms: Semantics, Culture, and Cognition', *Cognitive Linguistics*, 1–1 (1990), 99–150.

68   *Color*

39. Rolf G. Kuehni, 'Color Spaces and Color Order Systems', in *Color Ontology and Color Science*, ed. by Jonathan Cohen and Mohan Mathen (Cambridge: MIT Press, 2010), Chapter 1, pp. 3–36.
40. John Lyons, 'Colour in Language', in *Colour Art & Science*, ed. by Trevor Lamb and Janine Bourria (Cambridge: Cambridge University Press, 1995), Chapter 8, pp. 195–223.
41. *Color and Light in Ancient and Medieval Art*, ed. by Chloë N. Duckworth and Anne E. Sassin (London: Routledge, Taylor and Francis Group, 2018), p. 3.
42. Theo van Leeuwen, *The Language of Color – An Introduction* (London: Routledge, Taylor and Francis Group, 2011), p. 3.
43. Ibid, p. 16.
44. Ibid, pp. 43–44.
45. Brent Berlin and Paul Kay, *Basic Color Terms: Their Universality and Evolution* (Stanford: SLI Publications, 1999).
46. John Gage, 'Chapter 5 – Color-Language, Color Symbols', in *Color and Culture – Practice and Meaning from Antiquity to Abstraction* (Berkeley: University of California Press, 1993), p. 79.
47. Anna Wierzbicka, 'The Meaning of Color Terms: Semantics, Culture, and Cognition', *Cognitive Linguistics*, 1–1 (1990), 99–150.
48. Noud W. H. van Kruysbergen, Anna N. T. Bosman and Charles de Weert, 'Universal Colour Perception Versus Contingent Colour Naming: A Paradox?', *Behavioral and Brain Sciences*, 20.2 (1997), 209–210.
49. John Gage, 'Colour and Culture', in *Colour Art & Science*, ed. by Trevor Lamb and Janine Bourria (Cambridge: Cambridge University Press, 1995), Chapter 8, p. 188.
50. Bruno Latour, *Pandora's Hope* (Cambridge: Harvard University Press, 1999), pp. 58–60.
51. John Gage, 'Chapter 5 – Color-Language, Color Symbols', in *Color and Culture – Practice and Meaning from Antiquity to Abstraction* (Berkeley: University of California Press, 1993), p. 79.
52. Ibid.
53. Jan K. Koenderink, 'Colour, Old Age, and Accepted Truth', *Perception*, 28 (1999), 1–4.
54. Michael Tye, 'The Puzzle of True Blue', *Analysis*, 66.3 (2006), 173–178.
55. Michael Tye, 'The Truth About True Blue', *Analysis*, 66.4 (2006), 340–344.
56. John Gage, 'Introduction', in *Color and Culture – Practice and Meaning from Antiquity to Abstraction* (Berkeley: University of California Press, 1993), p. 10.
57. Fritz Hansen, 'Colors in Perfect Shape by Tal R', Online Video Recording, YouTube. <www.youtube.com/watch?v=3eVTGnn7y-c> [accessed 15 January 2023].
58. Evan Thompson, *Colour Vision – A Study in Cognitive Science and the Philosophy of Perception* (London: Routledge, 1995), p. 148.
59. Barbara Y. Ling and Sephe J. Dain, 'Color Vision in Children and the Lanthony New Color Test', *Visual Neuroscience*, 25 (2008), 441–444.
60. Evan Thompson, *Colour Vision – A Study in Cognitive Science and the Philosophy of Perception* (London: Routledge, 1995), p. 109.
61. David Katz, *The World of Color*, trans. by Robert B. MacLeod and Charles W. Fox (Oxfordshire: Routledge, 1935, reprinted 1999), pp. 7-12, 51–55.
62. Joel Pokorny, Steven K. Shevell and Vivianne C. Smith, 'Colour Appearance and Colour Constancy', in *The Perception of Colour*, ed. by Peter Gouras (London: The Macmillan Press, 1991), chapter 4, pp. 43–61.

63. Jamie Ward, *The Frog Who Croaked Blue – Synesthesia and the Mixing of the Senses* (London: Routledge, Taylor and Francis Group, 2008).

64. Richard E. Cytowic, David M. Eagleman and Dimitri Nabokov, *Wednesday Is Indigo Blue: Discovering the Brain of Synesthesia* (Cambridge: The MIT Press, 2011).

65. David Turbet, 'What Is Color-Blindness', (2022). <www.aao.org/eye-health/diseases/what-is-color-blindness> [accessed 2 May 2023].

66. Ricardo Bernardez-Vilaboa, 'The Implication of Vision and Colour in Cultural Heritage', *Heritage*, 3 (2020), 1063–1068. <https://doi.org/10.3390/heritage3040058>

67. Jamie Ward, *The Frog Who Croaked Blue – Synesthesia and the Mixing of the Senses* (London: Routledge, Taylor and Francis Group, 2008), pp. xii, 25.

68. Ibid, pp. 3–4.

69. Agnes Brokerhof, 'Spread or Sacrifice: Dilemma for Lighting Policies', *Studies in Conservation*, 63.suppl (2018), 28–34. <https://doi.org/10.1080/00393630.2018.1504439>

70. William McIlhagga, 'Colour Vision', in *The Colour Image Processing Handbook*, ed. by Stephen J. Sangwine and R. E. N. Horne (London: Chapman & Hall, 1998), Chapter 2, p. 21.

71. Theo van Leeuwen, *The Language of Color – An Introduction* (London: Routledge, Taylor and Francis Group, 2011), pp. 97–98.

72. Ibid, pp. 51, 52.

73. Ibid, p. 21.

74. John B. Best, *Cognitive Psychology*, 3rd edn (St. Paul: West Publishing, 1992), Chapter 3, pp. 82–127.

75. Ibid, p. 106.

76. Erik Rietveld and Julian Kiverstein, 'A Rich Landscape of Affordances', *Ecological Psychology*, 26 (2014), 325–352.

77. Roy S. Berns, *Color Science and the Visual Arts – A Guide for Conservators, Creators and the Curious* (Los Angeles: Getty Conservation Institute, 2016), pp. 33–34.

78. Faber Birren, *Color Perception in Art* (Atglen: Schiffer Publishing, 1986), p. 109.

79. Evan Thompson, *Colour Vision – A Study in Cognitive Science and the Philosophy of Perception* (London: Routledge, 1995).

80. Ibid, p. 104.

81. M. Baxandall, *Patterns of Intention: On the Historical Explanation of Pictures* (New Haven: Yale University Press, 1985), p. 45.

82. Jonathan Cohen, 'It's Not Easy Being Green: Hardin and Color Relationalism', in *Color Ontology and Color Science* (Cambridge: Massachusetts Institute of Technology, 2010), Chapter 5, pp. 123–147.

83. Evan Thompson, *Colour Vision – A Study in Cognitive Science and the Philosophy of Perception* (London: Routledge, 1995), pp. 109, 119-120.

84. Michael H. Brill, 'Color Constancy and Color Rendering: Concomitant Engineering of Illuminants and Reflectances', *Color Research and Application*, 13.3 (1988), 174–179.

85. Evan Thompson, *Colour Vision – A Study in Cognitive Science and the Philosophy of Perception* (London: Routledge, 1995), p. 43.

86. David H. Foster, 'Does Colour Constancy Exist?', *Trends in Cognitive Sciences*, 7.10 (2003), 439–443.

87. Faber Birren, 'Color Perception in Art Beyond the Eye into the Brain', *Leonardo*, 9.2 (1976), 105–110 (p. 107).

88. Faber Birren, *Color Perception in Art* (Atglen: Schiffer Publishing, 1986), pp. 48–49.
89. Rainer Mausfeld, 'Color within an Internalist Framework: The Role of 'Color' in the Structure of the Perceptual System', in *Color Ontology and Color Science*, ed. by Jonathan Cohen and Mohan Mathen (Cambridge: MIT Press, 2010), Chapter 5, pp. 123–147.
90. Ibid, p. 125.
91. Rainer Mausfeld, 'The Perception of Material Qualities and the Internal Semantics of the Perceptual System', in *Perception Beyond Inference. The Information Content of Visual Processes*, ed. by Liliana Albertazzi and others (Cambridge: MIT Press, 2011), pp. 159–200.
92. Joseph J. Sheppard, Jr., *Human Color Perception – A Critical Study of the Experimental Foundation* (New York: American Elsevier Publishing Company, 1968), p. 35.
93. Faber Birren, *Color Perception in Art* (Atglen: Schiffer Publishing, 1986), p. 24.
94. Jonathan Westphal, 'How Can the Logic of Colo Concepts Apply to Afterimage Colors', in *Color Ontology and Color Science*, ed. by Jonathan Cohen and Mohan Mathen (Cambridge: MIT Press, 2010), pp. 245–255.
95. W. (Bill) Wei and IJsbrand Hummelen, *Unpublished Research* (Amsterdam: Cultural Heritage Agency of the Netherlands, 2017).

4 Surface texture and appearance

Even though an object may be reproduced in "true color" using digital or print media, experience shows that the reproduction still doesn't look real. What is missing is the third dimension, in particular, on a microscopic scale. This third dimension, the roughness of an object surface, is what determines whether an object is glossy or matt. The surface roughness also provides microscopic shadowing effects which provide the viewer with a sense of texture as well as providing the human perception system with cues as to subtleties of changes in the third dimension.

In industry, techniques for measuring and quantifying roughness have been used since the middle of the previous century. In this chapter, the introduction of such "objective" measurements into conservation science will be discussed and, as with color, juxtaposed with subjective judgments of appearance, in particular, of gloss and matteness. A number of techniques for roughness measurement will be introduced, including macroscopic tools based on raking light photography, to industrial and research grade profilometry down to almost atomic scales. Several case studies will be discussed, showing the usefulness of these techniques, but again questioning as to how much detail is really necessary for practical conservation work.

4.1 The "real" appearance of things

While giving an annual lecture on perception to university conservation students, the author shows them several images of two-dimensional works of art using Microsoft PowerPoint™. An image of Vincent van Gogh's *Wheatfield with Crows* (1890), Fig. 4.1, elicits responses mostly related to the bright contrasting colors, but nothing at all is said about the strong impasto, the thick brush strokes with which Van Gogh worked. An image of John Russell's portrait of John Collin of Devizes (1799), Fig. 4.2, always elicits a description of an oil painting technique which provides a soft, matt appearance to the image, although the work is actually a pastel painting.

One can further ask what one is looking at when one sees a PowerPoint™ or printed image of a three-dimensional object, for example, what looks like

DOI: 10.4324/9781003217800-4

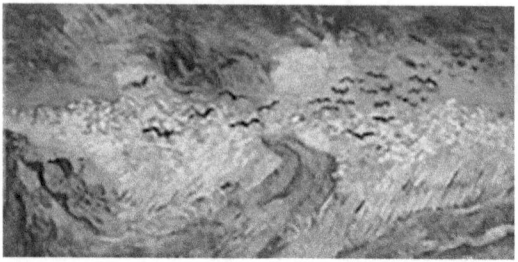

Fig. 4.1 Digital image of Vincent van Gogh's *Wheatfield with Crows* (1890). The impasto used is not evident in such a flat two-dimensional image.

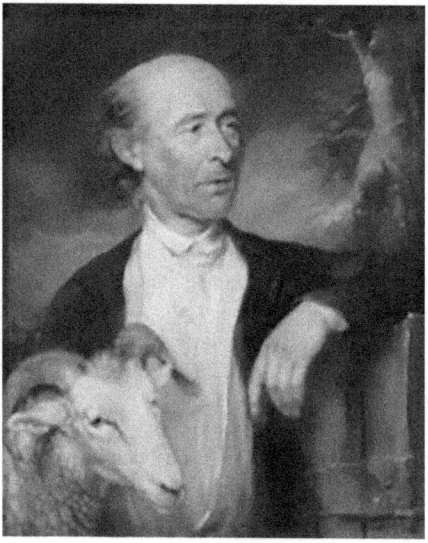

Fig. 4.2 Digital image John Russell's portrait of John Collin of Devizes (1799). Virtually all people who are asked about this image mistake it for an oil painting. It is, in fact, a pastel painting.

a flower vase. If one sees the elliptical base of a flower vase in a photograph, most people will assume based on experience that it has some cylindrical form, perhaps not symmetric, but certainly rounded on the side hidden from the viewer. But is that true? They may not be too surprised if it had a handle on the side hidden from the viewer and was actually a water pitcher, or find it humorous if the other side were perfectly flat. The point is that the three-dimensional aspect of a photograph of a three-dimensional object is completely lost. As Gombrich [1] and Koenderink [2] have pointed out, there are an infinite number of possibilities of how a 3D object could be perceived if viewed in a two-dimensional image, for example, the "Ames chair illusions."

The same issue arises for images of two-dimensional works of art or, more generally speaking, for images of the surfaces of works of art. What one sees in real life is not purely a two-dimensional color reproduction. The surfaces of works of art all have some sort of texture or, in more technical terms, roughness. The appearance of objects is therefore not solely determined by color, but in combination with the surface texture/roughness or micro-roughness of their surfaces. With regard to the two examples of paintings presented above, it is the micro-roughness of a surface which determines its degree of gloss or matteness. In fact, a number of well-known artists including Max Beckmann and Claude Monet, and the Cubists including George Braques and Pablo Picasso, specifically did not want their paintings varnished because they did not want the gloss to take away the surface effects they were trying to achieve. Surface roughness also causes the object to change in appearance due to micro-shadowing effects depending on how light is reflected from it, and not only in terms of the perception of the colors as discussed in the previous chapter. The use of thick brush strokes, impasto, provides a coarse third dimension to, for example, a Van Gogh painting. Van Leeuwen notes that one of the essential characteristics of Van Gogh's color scheme is actually 'the modulation created by the visible brush strokes which intermingle lighter and darker values of the same color, or adjacent colors such as yellow and green" [3]. The roughness of a surface also imparts a visual sense of how an object physically may feel.

Measuring the physical properties of surfaces and trying to reproduce them is actually a field where conservation science is lagging behind industrial engineering and design in terms of techniques for measuring gloss and surface roughness, and relating that to the perception of works of art. Art historical research combined with such techniques could have much more to say about how artist's physical techniques (e.g. brush strokes, carving or polishing) influence appearance using subjective terms such as gloss and matteness, softness, and velvet texture. In the following sections, measurement technologies will first be examined, which are in themselves not new, but have been recently introduced in art conservation. These include how the gloss and micro-roughness of surfaces can be measured. Just as with other scientific instrumentation, these methods provide quantitative "objective" results. However, what they mean in terms of what people see is again a question of perception.

4.2   Gloss measurements

Throughout history, gloss or the lack thereof has played an important role in how things are perceived. Things that are glossy, shiny, or glittery have almost always been considered to be valuable in some way. One only needs to think of the perceived value of objects made of precious metals such as gold, silver, or platinum; precious stones such as diamonds, sapphires, and rubies; and textiles such as satin. In modern times, this concept of value is also translated into, for example, metallic paint on automobiles, highly polished chrome finishes, and the use of furniture polishes. On the other hand, matteness is also considered by many to be just as important, providing a feeling of elegance or a subdued contrast against all of the glitter and gloss.

Glossiness and matteness can also affect appearance in a negative manner. Many varnished paintings are difficult to view in museums because of specular reflection, the annoying bright speckled area on those paintings illuminated using spotlights. Dust makes objects look more matt, which has created an interesting debate in historic English buildings as to whether dusty interiors provide a sense of age, or just show that the building just isn't properly cared for [4, 5].

The scientific principle of glossiness or matteness is described schematically in Fig. 4.3. If a ray of light is projected onto a surface at a given angle, θ, and completely reflects to an observer at the same angle, the surface is

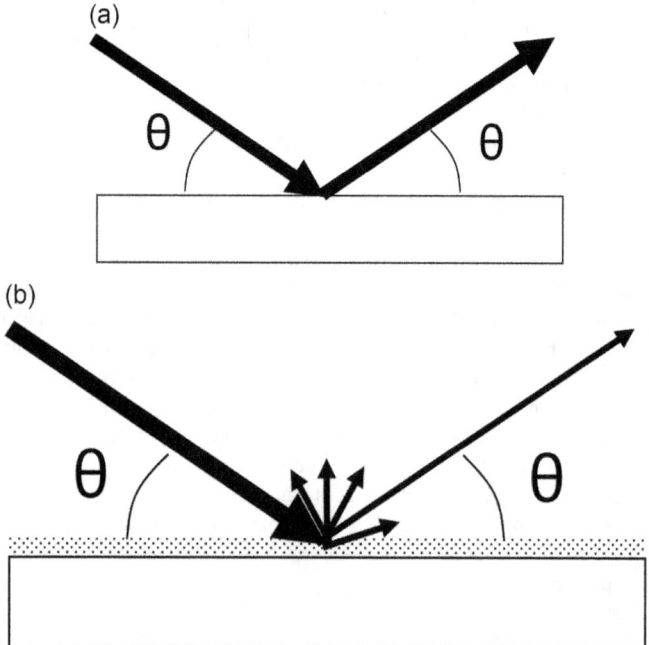

Fig. 4.3 Schematic diagram showing the reflection of a ray of light on a
a) 100% glossy surface
b) matt surface

considered to be 100% glossy, Fig. 4.3a. If the surface has some roughness, the light ray will be scattered to some extent so that not all of the light will reflect at the same angle (Fig. 4.3b). The observer will therefore not see all of the reflected light, and the surface is then considered to be matt. The degree of matteness depends on how rough the surface is – the rougher the surface, the more light scatters in other directions than the angle, θ.

The glossiness of a surface can be measured with commercially available, standardized instruments known as glossmeters. Glossmeters are used for quality control, in particular, for consumer products which require consistent appearance. For example, if one wants to purchase a new automobile with a metallic blue color, the "metallic" will have been defined as a certain gloss value measured and quantified by a glossmeter. It should be obvious that if a dealer has five of the same model automobile in metallic blue, they should all look the same in terms of gloss and color under the same lighting conditions.

Glossmeters work based on the principle which was described using Fig. 4.3. A simple glossmeter has a light beam source which illuminates the surface at a given angle, θ. Commercial instruments are available for measuring at 20°, 60°, or 85°. More expensive versions have a combination of two or all three angles. A detector is positioned at the same angle, θ, opposite to the light source. If a surface is perfectly glossy, all of the light produced by the light source will be seen by the detector, and the glossmeter will indicate 100% gloss. The rougher the surface, the less light will be reflected into the detector at angle θ. The glossmeter will indicate this as a value less than 100% gloss. Most commercially available glossmeters make use of so-called gloss units (GU), where 100% gloss is defined as 1000 or 2000 GUs. This allows for more resolution in the gloss measurement.

A note of caution is that the comparison of gloss measurements can only be directly made for surfaces with the same reflectance spectra (color). A darker colored surface, that is, one which absorbs more light, will reflect less light than a lighter colored surface. The glossmeter will therefore return a lower gloss unit measurement, even though the surface roughness of both surfaces might be the same. One therefore cannot directly compare the surface roughness of specimens with different colors, nor determine changes of gloss of a specimen that has aged if it has strongly discolored during the aging process.

The question, as has already been asked and will continue to be asked in this book in relation to other scientific measurement techniques, is as follows: what does the gloss measurement mean? In fact, as a stand-alone number, the gloss measurement does not mean anything. Unlike in color science where there is at least some sort of culturally determined relationship between reflectance spectra and color language, there are no words to describe, say 362 GUs or 859 GUs. However, one can say that a surface with a gloss measurement value of 859 GUs is glossier than a surface with 362 GUs. Gloss measurements are thus comparative in nature. One can only say that one surface is glossier or more matt than the other.

Whether a surface is glossy or not compared to a more matt surface, and whether that is acceptable or not, is the subjective decision of the viewer. In the automobile example above, the gloss value for metallic blue is based on a comparison with some standard metallic blue specimen, which a committee of humans selected as having the desired appearance. As will be discussed in one of the case studies in Section 4.4, gloss measurements looking at dust in museums are based solely on what the museum professionals involved considered "too dusty." "Objective" gloss measurements returned by a glossmeter must therefore be attached to a subjective human perception judgment about the glossiness of the surface. For the purposes of art conservation, when conducting gloss measurements in order to determine the effect, for example, of a certain treatment, perception testing should always be conducted, and that on a (sample) surface of realistic size. One should also be aware of the limits in precision of a gloss measurement. A glossmeter may detect a minute change, say 2 GU in 1000, which may be a cause of concern to some conservators. The question is, however, whether a viewer can even notice that change within the margins of error for such measurements, namely, one to two GUs.

While gloss measurements are therefore a useful tool for providing some quantitative measure of changes in appearance of a work of art after it has been treated, they are macroscopic in nature. In order to determine what is causing the change in gloss, one needs to determine what has physically happened to the surface roughness, the property which determines gloss in the first place. The innovative use of surface roughness measurement techniques is beginning to shed more light on (pun not intended) the effects of (chemical) treatments on the physical properties of the surfaces of works of art.

4.3   Roughness measurements

When the author first entered the conservation field, he was talking to a paintings conservator about cleaning. The conservator was concerned that the painting he had just cleaned, that is, from which he had just removed the varnish, looked matt. The author thought, of course it does, you just removed the varnish. But in time, he learned that that was not the concern. The concern was that artists had known for centuries that varnishes worked best if they had the same or similar optical properties to the binder of the paint which the varnish covered, in particular, the property which is now known technically as the index of refraction. Thus, what the conservator was worried about was that the treatment he had used had not only removed the varnish but had also begun to remove the binder of the paint layer immediately below. Thus, the paint layer was more matt than he had expected.

In the past, the initial response to such questions was based on chemical analysis. It is, however, now known that what the conservator was concerned about was not a result of the change in roughness due to the removal of the varnish itself, but the additional change in roughness due to the possible removal of binder from the paint. The remaining pigment particles would then stand out higher on the surface, increasing its roughness, and thus its matteness.

The modern-day measurement of surface roughness, technically known as surface profilometry, has been in use since the first half to mid-20th century. Profilometry and the study of surface roughness is an important part of the engineering science of tribology, the study of friction, wear, and lubrication.

Techniques for the measurement of surface roughness, that is, profilometry, have been commercially available since the mid-1950s. The first profilometers under the trade name Talysurf™ made use of a diamond needle/stylus, much like that of an old phonograph needle, which was then drawn across the surface. One thus obtained a line profile, which reminds one of current-day profiles of a stage through the mountains of the famous Tour de France bicycle race. In fact, such a profile is actually a roughness line profile of the earth along the route of the stage. Besides a visualization of the surface roughness, quantitative data can be obtained by calculating various statistical parameters of the profile. Useful internationally standardized parameters for works of art include the average roughness, R_a, the mathematical average of all peaks and valleys about a mean line in absolute value (no negative or positive sign), and Rq, the so-called root-mean-square value which is more sensitive to height variations.

There are two disadvantages to such contact profilometers, especially for studying works of art. First, a line profile says very little about the full or even just a part of a surface that a viewer is looking at. One can scan several lines next to each other to produce a three-dimensional surface profile, but with such stylus profilometers, it is extremely time-consuming, and the spatial resolution of a physical stylus depends on the radius of the stylus tip, which is often larger than the roughness effect one is trying to measure. Furthermore, the use of a diamond needle is, of course, a contact measurement which can damage the surface of the object, something not desirable in art conservation. Similar issues have had to be dealt with for the quality control of industrial parts and products.

A major innovation which solved those problems was the development of contactless profilometry in the first two decades of the 21st century using specially adapted confocal laser or white-light profilometers. The working principle is essentially what one does with a light microscope when trying to examine a very rough surface. One cannot focus on everything at once, so one turns a knob and moves the objective lens up and down to focus on different levels of the surface. This up-and-down motion is nothing more than a height measurement. Through the use of special imaging optics and computer-controlled micro-motors, a confocal profilometer takes a series of images as the objective lens moves up (or down) [6, 7], for example, of a cleaned acrylic paint sample (see Fig. 4.4a). By blocking the unfocused parts of the image using a special aperture, the profilometer essentially collects a set of focused contours, each contour being at a particular height (see Fig. 4.4b). By adding all of these contours together, one then obtains a completely focused image of the rough surface, in this case, of a cleaned acrylic paint sample. In addition, because each of the contours is associated with a specific vertical position of the objective lens, one can color-code this image to obtain a map of the surface with quantitative height information, analogous to a topographic map for hiking or geographic studies (see Fig. 4.4c). When analyzing the data, one can also easily obtain line profiles. In Fig. 4.4d, one sees a line profile across the middle of the specimen, line in Fig. IV.4a, which says something about the

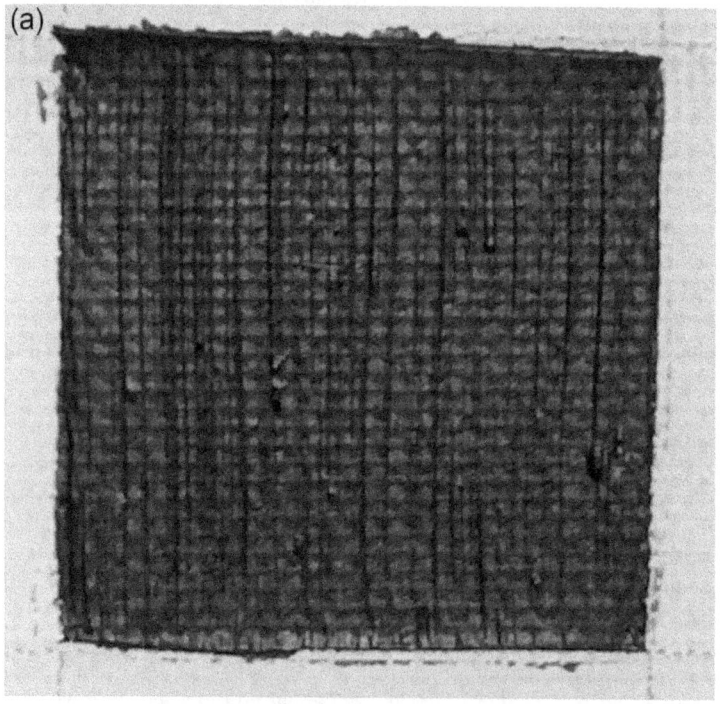

Fig. 4.4 A noncontact confocal white light profilometer collects from

a) an acrylic paint sample

b) a set of contours at each height of the objective lens, adding them together to provide

c) a focused image of a cleaned acrylic paint sample which can be quantitatively color coded into a three-dimensional false-color topographic map of a surface (red is high through yellow, green to blue which is low)

d) line profile across the specimen (line in c) showing waviness

e) expanding line profile in c), from 0.98 to 1.07 mm, to show micro-roughness

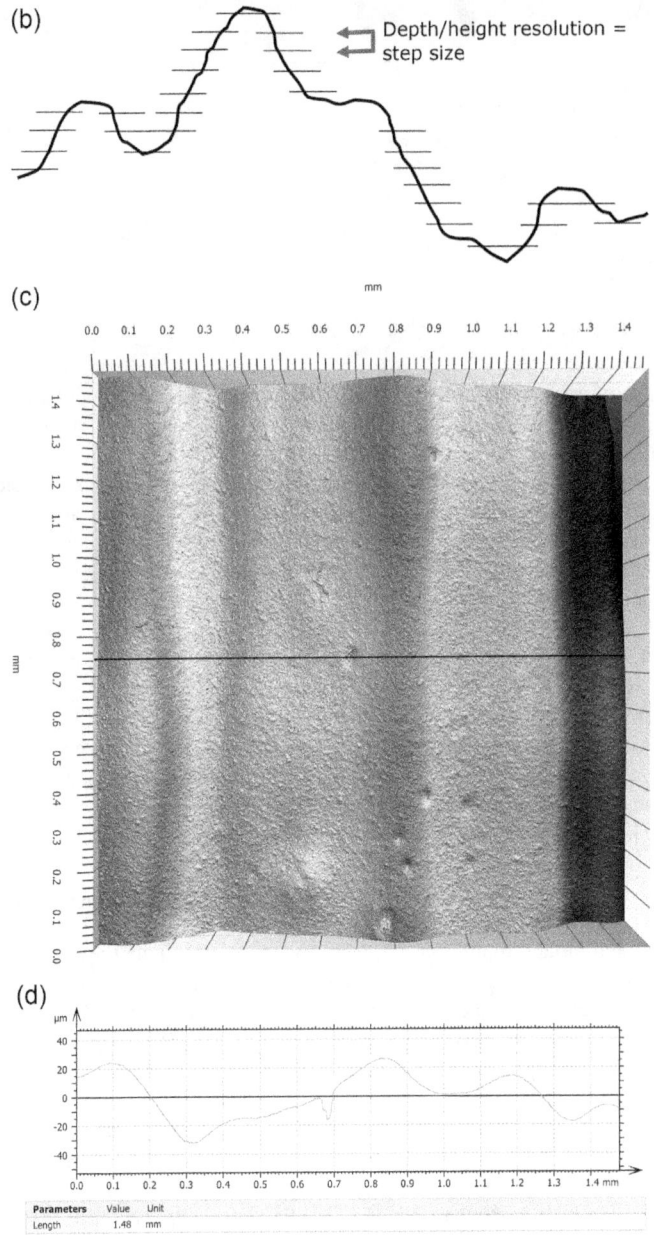

(b)

Depth/height resolution = step size

(c)

mm

mm

(d)

Parameters	Value	Unit
Length	1.48	mm

Fig. 4.4 (Continued)

(e)

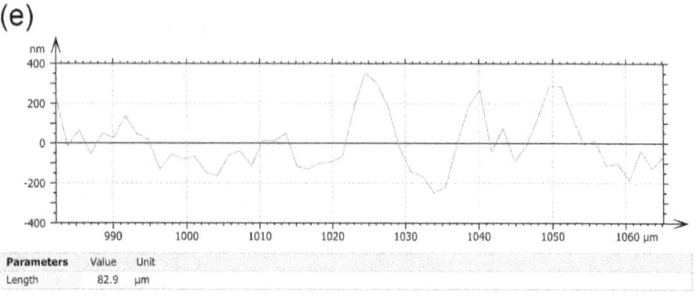

Parameters	Value	Unit
Length	82.9	μm

Fig. 4.4 (Continued)

degree of impasto. One can also expand the profile, for example, in the "valley" between 0.98 and 1.07 mm, to obtain the micro-roughness which can be changed by a conservation treatment (see Fig. 4.4e).

Besides the fact that it is a high-resolution, contactless measurement system, the advantages of commercially available confocal profilometers are that one can measure areas of several square millimeters in less than 10 minutes, with roughness (height) resolutions down to 30 nanometers. Note that the spatial resolution is the same as for a normal light microscope, that is, the wavelength of light, less than 1 μm. Since the objective lens can only cover a certain area, one can measure several contiguous areas and digitally "stitch" them together. One can thus measure larger areas which are recognizable to the naked eye (see Fig. 4.4c). One can also obtain the equivalent roughness parameters discussed for line profiles above, but then for surfaces, including average surface roughness, S_a, and one can go back to exactly the same location to, for example, examine an object/surface before and after a conservation treatment. One company uses blue light as its light source, which then offers a spatial resolution of around 0.4 μm. It should be noted that a further advantage of confocal profilometers is that one can measure in air, as opposed to having to place the specimen or object in the vacuum of a scanning electron microscope (SEM).

A step further in profilometry, which has seen some initial use recently in cultural heritage research, is atomic-force microscopy (AFM) (e.g,. [8, 9]). AFM makes use of a micro-stylus to measure the surface topography at nanometer scale, that is, on the order of several atom diameters. Detecting the positions of atoms or groups of atoms in the early stages of surface reactions is of particular importance in the study and development of nano-technology for computer chip technology, catalytic convertors, in cell biology, and in corrosion research.

Again, while these are interesting and potentially useful techniques, the question again arises as to why one needs to study works of art at such microscopic to atomic levels. Proper interpretation is essential in the use of any surface science techniques, but care is especially necessary in interpreting the results in terms of daily conservation practice, and in light of the time frame of what one calls cultural heritage. In Section 4.5, a case study is discussed concerning possible scratching of Plexiglas™ during conservation treatments. It was found using optical microscopy that certain treatments apparently caused deep scratches in the material. However, when those specimens were examined using confocal with light profilometry, it was found that the scratches were only 30 to 50 nm deep, and essentially not visible to the naked eye when viewing the real object.

If one then considers AFM, with roughness levels on the order of one nanometer, one can really question whether anyone can see that, much less whether the information has any application when considering conservation at bulk material levels. For example, Marquardt and others [8] looked at nano-coatings for preventing the tarnishing of silver objects, claiming promising results. Aside from the fact that in terms of conservation ethics, the use of a coating is seldom allowed, tarnishing is less of a problem in current properly climatized museums than it used to be. Furthermore, a look at the vast academic and industrial corrosion literature would show that, in practice, such thin coatings necessary for heritage objects always have defects and thus would not prevent the initiation of tarnishing. At the other end of the cultural heritage time scale, Barberio and others [9] used AFM to study the removal of patina from archaeological stone using laser ablation. It is questionable why one would use an instrument for measuring atomic layers when one is blasting away several tens to hundreds of nanometers of material, which in of itself cannot be reasonably studied using AFM.

4.4   Texture mapping and 3D microscopy

While profilometry gives a precise quantitative description of the surface roughness of a specimen, that information may not always be necessary, and, in any case, the instrumentation is not affordable for the average conservator. Parallel with developments in profilometry, a number of techniques were developed to provide more inexpensive solutions for visualizing 3D surfaces.

A number of these techniques involve the use of raking light, including a technique known as polynomial texture mapping (PTM). PTM was developed by one of the original computer hardware manufacturers, Hewlett Packard, in the 1980s. Besides industrial applications, it was used for the imaging of cultural heritage beginning at the end of this century [10, 11]. It involves the use of raking light at various angles to produce more realistic images of three-dimensional objects, and also to elicit shadows on a surface in order to study the surface texture. A PTM image is obtained by placing an object under a hemispheric frame with a camera at the top (see schematic diagram in Fig. 4.5). A series of lights are arranged in an array around the object at different levels of the dome. The object is then photographed with each light on, one by one. The result is a set of raking light images taken at different angles of illumination. Software programs combine the images so that users can view the objects under different lighting conditions as if they were moving the light source around. Furthermore, the

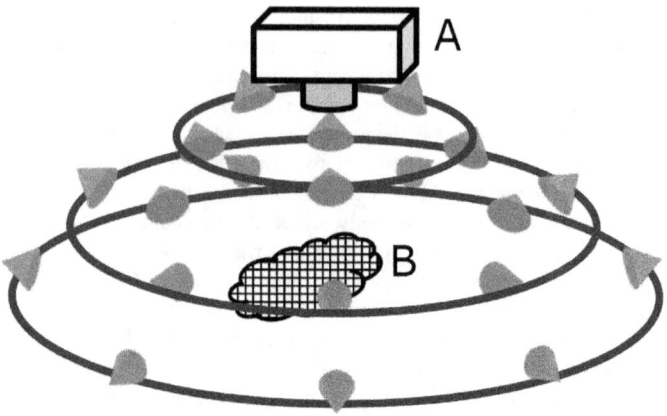

Fig. 4.5 Schematic diagram of the set-up for polynomial texture mapping with camera (A) at the top, and lights (cone shapes) mounted on a dome at different angles to photograph object (B).

surface texture can be calculated based on the geometry of the imaging system and the shadows cast by the surface of the object.

A variation on this technique, edge reflection analysis, uses the reflection of polarized light at different angles to determine the topography of the surface. This technique was used, for example, by Pollmeier and Arney for determining the surface texture of photograph papers [12]. A light ray shining on a rough surface will only reflect spectrally in a particular direction, as was discussed for gloss (see Section 4.2). A viewer or detector will then only see spots of light for rays which happen to be at the same angle as from the light ray. If the position of the light ray is changed, the spots of light will change position, since the angle at which the light hits the surface texture feature changes. Note that this is the same effect as one sees when looking at the sparkling of water from the waves of the ocean at sunset [13], only in that case, the light source, the sun, remains more or less fixed, at least within the time frame of wave movement. By systematically changing the angle at which the light hits the surface, one can calculate the surface angles of all of the microfeatures of the surface, and then their heights. The angle at which the sunlight hits the waves changes because of the wave movement, and spots of light thus seem to move around. Calculations of surface texture on photographs were reported to have a resolution of 0.5 millimeters (mm), that is, 50 μm, which is poor in comparison to profilometer resolutions.

There have also been developments in optical microscopy using the stepwise focusing technique described previously for confocal profilometry. So-called 3D digital microscopy provides users with magnified (color) images of rough surfaces or small components which can be manipulated so that one can examine the surfaces of the objects as one is physically handling them. While this is useful, they do not provide the roughness data that a true profilometer does, and the advertised resolutions and magnifications are based on inter-polated values. As such, they provide improved visualization of objects over normal stereo and optical microscopes, but not the true magnification that many users in cultural heritage had hoped for.

4.5   Case studies

As with color science, the use of the "objective" science of tribology in art conservation is also fraught with issues of the subjective interpretation of the results. The debate as to whether a change in gloss or matteness of, for exam-ple, a historic piece of wood furniture is acceptable in a conservation treatment is similar to the debate on changes in spectral reflection after the cleaning of a painting. Both are influenced by the background, viewing position, and pro-fessional preferences of the viewer. A conservation treatment may result in a change in surface roughness on a micro- or nanoscale. The question is, how-ever, whether the resulting change in gloss or matteness is even visible to the naked eye. Furthermore, the question can also be raised, at least for objects in strictly controlled museum climates, as to how much they will visibly change in appearance in, say, the next two or three generations. A number of case studies, some from the author's own research, are now presented to show the difficulty of weighing objectively measured surface properties against profes-sional and personal perception in conservation decision-making.

4.5.1   Surface changes due to conservation treatments

One of the earliest mentions of noncontact profilometry for use in conserva-tion, which the author has found, was work conducted in Germany toward the end of the previous century, using laser profilometry to determine the effect of tensides on the surface of oil paints [14]. It was then recognized that the surface roughness could be quantified according to international industrial standards, an advantage compared to scanning electron microscopy. The laser profilometer used at that time could measure a line profile. A three-dimen-sional topographical image could be built up by measuring a series of parallel line scans. However, the spatial resolution at the time was poor (50 µm), as was the depth resolution (1 µm). It also took up to 24 hours to measure a sur-face area of 4 x 4 mm, an area easily found on an object with the naked eye.

At the turn of the 21st century, this author began using confocal profilom-etry for investigating the effect of conservation treatments on acrylic paint-ings, wall paintings, and plastics. These studies were conducted with a spatial resolution of 1–2 µm and a depth resolution from 30 to 100 nm, depending on which objective lens was used. Areas of 2 x 2 mm could be measured in a matter of minutes, though rougher surfaces took somewhat longer.

A major concern for paintings conservators is the cleaning of water-sensitive acrylic paints. A study was therefore carried out to investigate the effect of dry-cleaning on the roughness of such paints. A comparison before and after false-color topographic images of acrylic paint samples at the same location showed, for example, that cleaning with a cotton swab and distilled water removed dust particles from an acrylic paint sample surface without changing the roughness of the paint surface, at the 0.1 μm depth resolution available for profilometry at the time [15]. On the other hand, it was found that using a dry sponge resulted in the deposit of several particles of the sponge, with only slight changes in the higher parts of the paint sample. Viewed with the naked eye, no difference in appearance between samples with these and several other cleaning methods could be seen, except for a more aggressive treatment with acetone.

Another example of the use of profilometry for paintings was a study of various coatings used to protect the surface of wall paintings when they are removed and transferred to another substrate using the so-called strappo technique [16]. Several coatings were successful in the sense that no paint loss was found after the treatment. However, white-light confocal profilometry showed that the cloth which is pressed into the paint surface in order to lift it does leave impressions of one to five μm in depth in the paint layer. Given the roughness of the original wall painting surface, these impressions were not visible to the naked eye.

A final example is a project which was conducted in order to determine the effect of cleaning on the surface condition of face-mounted photographs as well as other objects made of polymethylmethacrylate (PMMA), including Plexiglas™ and Perspex™. The cleaning of such materials is difficult because of their sensitivity to chemicals and scratching. Face-mounted photographs consist of a sheet of Plexiglas™ glued to the surface of a photograph to saturate the colors ("wet-look") and provide an illusion of depth [15, 17]. An investigation into the cleaning of face-mounted photographs was conducted, where 12 cleaning methods were used up to 100 times on specimens to simulate 100 annual cleanings. The results indicated that scratching occurred on samples which had been dry-cleaned using a number of methods. These scratches were quite visible under the light microscope. However, when the roughness of the surfaces of the same specimens was measured using confocal profilometry, the scratches were found to be on the order of 30 to 50 nm deep. Furthermore, specimens which had been cleaned with nonaggressive liquids such as deionized water showed no scratching, but did indicate that some streaking during drying had taken place. The question was whether these microscopic changes in roughness could be seen.

This author [18] therefore conducted a perception test with professional and lay subjects using face-mounted photographs, with each photograph being half white and half black. Each specimen was cleaned using one of twelve different methods and then hung in different venues along with photographs which had not been treated. Subjects including the general public and conservation professionals at the Nederlands Fotomuseum, the Fotomuseum Antwerpen, and the Netherlands Institute for Cultural Heritage were simply asked to rank the quality of the photographs and give their reasons. The final result was that within the statistics of 110 participants, no one could tell the difference between the treatments. Given that many well-known face-mounted photographs by, for example, Andreas Gursky, Thomas Struth, or Thomas Ruff are up to several meters on a side [17], the question is, in fact, whether it matters which cleaning method one uses of the twelve given that there will only be the occasional sub-micrometer deep scratch in 100 years.

Such initial results of the use of confocal profilometry thus show that it is a useful technology for determining the effects of cleaning treatments on art materials. The results indicate that there are differences in the effect of various treatments on the surface roughness of test specimens. However, the results do beg the question as to whether such changes are important given that they are not visible to the naked eye, and that with a few exceptions such as Plexiglas, most works of art are not treated or cleaned (dust) anywhere close to annually as was simulated for the work on face-mounted photographs.

4.5.2 Identification of photo papers

An issue confronting photograph conservators is identifying the kind of photographic paper an artist used in printing the final product. A photographic paper is a collective term which includes both the paper or plastic substrate and the layer containing the photographic image itself. There are thousands of types of photographic papers with different visual characteristics and a confusing variety of names which, in some way, make use of the terms "matte" and "glossy." In order to properly treat a photographic work of art, a conservator must be able to identify the paper with which it was created. This is not always possible visually, and many papers lack manufacturer's markings.

The photographic conservation group under Paul Messier has been developing a database of the textures of photographic papers using PTM techniques [19]. The database also includes measurements of paper thickness, weight, and gloss. A difficulty that is being addressed is assisting conservators with automatically finding a match within the database for an unknown photographic paper [19, 20]. It is interesting to note that subjective descriptions are also being used in the database to help in identifying papers, by trying to standardize the semantics for their description of the appearance of the papers using terms such as warm/cold, semi-matte, or buff to their measurements [20].

This author and Stigter [21] demonstrated the problems of using subjective terms when trying to identify photographic papers. A pilot project was conducted for ranking the glossiness of photographic papers using roughness measurements, gloss measurements, and human perception testing. It was found that roughness measurements did not always correlate with gloss measurements as one might expect, and that human subjects could easily be confused by glossy surfaces which were visibly rough. In particular, photographic papers with a regular pattern of nubs which were clearly visible with the naked eye were problematic for the subjects, because, they saw the paper as glossy but, in their minds, knew that a regular pattern of nubs is "rough" (see roughness measurements in Fig. 4.6). Dr. W. (Bill) Wei

(a)

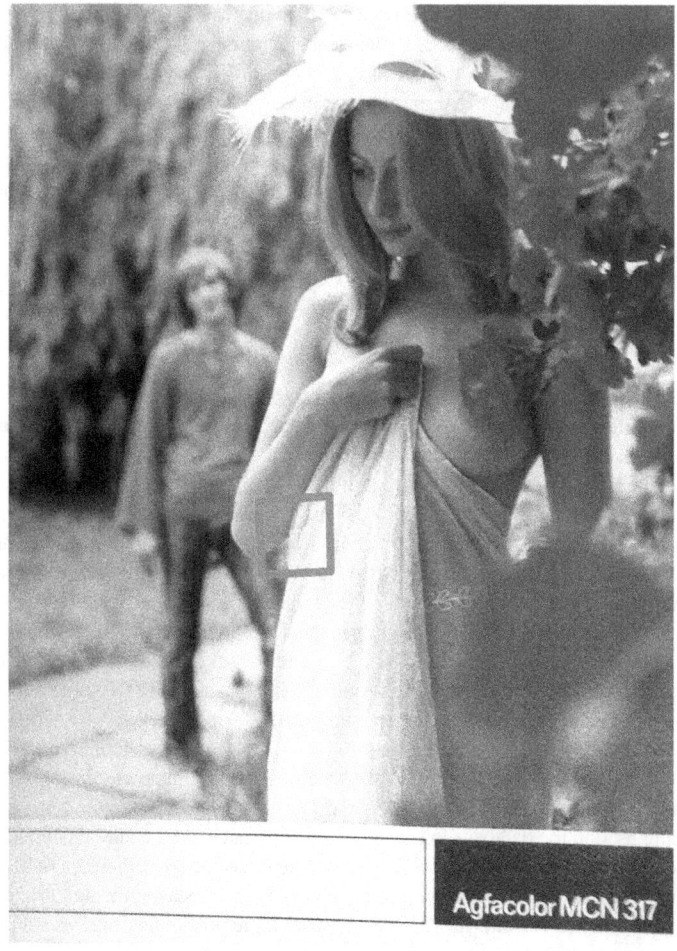

Fig. 4.6 Surface roughness of a 4.6 x 4.6 mm section of a photograph paper (Agfacolor MCN 317) which perception test subjects could not decide whether it was glossy or not due to its visible "nub" texture

a) Photograph

b) False-color topographic map of the measured area

(b)

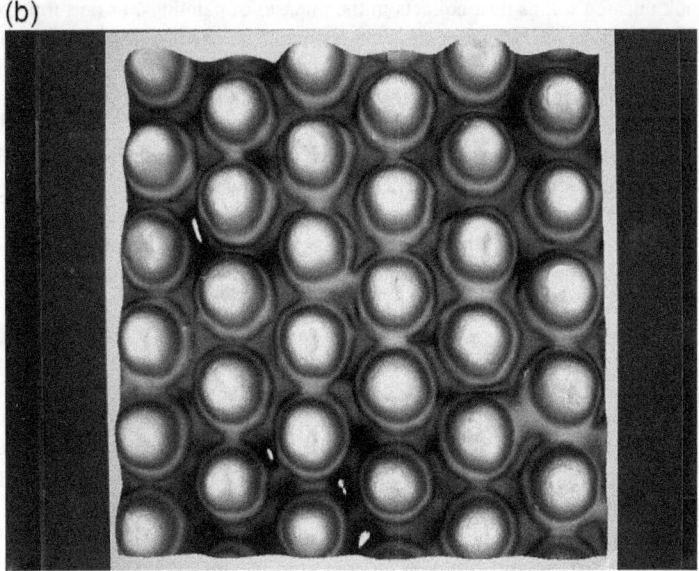

Fig. 4.6 (Continued)

has thus begun focusing on measuring the surface roughness of photographic papers, up to several square millimeters in minute, and creating a database of topographical false-color images and standardized roughness values for quantitatively describing the surface of the papers. By comparing roughness values of an unknown paper with the database, a conservator can narrow down the possibilities for identifying the paper and minimizing the need for subjective evaluation.

4.5.3 Dust in museums

A third example of the difficulty of using "objective" measurements to assist in subjective conservation decision-making deals with the problem of dust in museums. There are a number of problems associated with the collection of dust in museums. One is a technical issue, which the reader may have come across in his or her attic. In the humid climates of buildings without climate control, humidity can allow dust to cake onto the surface of object, and also lead to chemical reactions with the materials. Two other problems are subjective in nature. The first is the esthetic issue that, for most people, dust on an object does not look good. It changes the appearance of an object, for example, dulling glossy surfaces or bright colors, or making an object or collection look uncared for, as dust collects in the impasto of paintings, or on furniture in a historic house. The second is the economic issue of having to have collection managers clean entire collections regularly (see again [4]). The faster the dust collects to an unacceptable level, the more often museum staff must spend time to clean the collection.

The collection of dust can be monitored using gloss measurements, which were described in Section 4.2. The reader is reminded, however, that making a gloss measurement on a dusty surface gives a value (in GU), that in and of itself does not mean anything. Someone has to say whether that surface is too dusty. If the "too dusty" value is established, one can then conduct monitoring on freshly cleaned surfaces to determine when the surface, as reached the critical value.

It is often more useful to determine how fast dust collects so that one can better plan cleaning intervals. This author and his colleagues [5] describe a method for doing this, using measurements of the change of gloss of standard-sized glass slides used for optical microscopy. The slide is first cleaned, and then the gloss of the slide is measured on a white background, for example, photocopy paper. The slide is then placed at the location of interest, somewhere where it is free to collect dust, but not be disturbed by visitors. After roughly a month, the gloss of the slide, now with some dust, is again measured on the same white background. This is the change in gloss, a negative change, for that month. The slide is then cleaned, the gloss measured on the white background, and replaced at the location. Every month, the cumulative change is plotted in a graph, with the cumulative change in gloss on the vertical axis and the time on the horizontal axis (see, e.g., Fig. 4.7).

In the example, one sees plots for different locations in the Museum of Ethnography in Leiden, The Netherlands. This is a museum with a modern climate control system. One sees curves with different slopes. The steeper the curve, the faster dust collects at a certain location. The main entrance to the Museum of Ethnography and the Indonesia exhibition room, which is adjacent to it and often the way to special exhibitions, collects dust the fastest, while the conservation studios and the Maya exhibition room in one of the farthest reaches of the museum show the lowest rates of dust collection. These measurements confirm earlier findings [23, 24] that visitors are the largest source of dust.

These quantitative dust measurements also showed the perils of using a purely visual judgment for initially determining whether a location is too dusty. When the museum staff were asked to indicate locations which were considered too dusty, they did not identify what was actually one of the dustiest locations, a showcase with matte gray shelves [5]. This only became evident when an object was removed from one of the shelves and the clean spot under the object became clearly visible.

Museum Volkenkunde

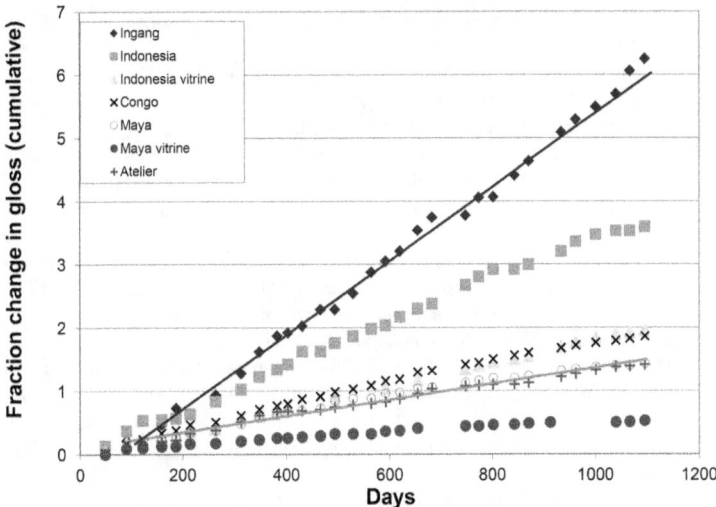

Fig. 4.7 Cumulative change in gloss due to the collection of dust in different rooms in a museum. Note that the vertical axis is an absolute value. The change is actually negative (loss of gloss due to dust accumulation) [22].

4.6 Summary of Chapter 4

In this chapter, the innovative use of roughness and gloss measurements for conservation was reviewed. It was shown that roughness measurements are useful for characterizing and documenting the surfaces of works of art, and for studying the effects of conservation treatments on surface condition. Roughness measurements can be conducted down to almost atomic levels. However, if some change due to a conservation treatment is found at that level, it cannot be seen by the human eye. Given that years or decades may pass before most objects are again treated, one can certainly ask what the significance of such atomic level changes is in the context of generations of preservation. Roughness measurements have been used to identify materials such as photographic papers. However, such measurements are only a guideline. The human eye is still required to make the final identification. Gloss measurements are a simple but important tool for determining changes in appearance in terms of glossiness or matteness. However, gloss measurements only can be used to determine changes in gloss, not absolute values. Determining what a proper gloss level is, is a subjective decision. A number of case studies were described, which show the limits of what innovations in roughness and gloss measurements can do in art conservation, limits posed by the subjectivity of human perception.

References

1. Ernst Gombrich, *Art and Illusion*, 6th edn (London: Phaidon Press, 2002), pp. 209–211.
2. Jan Koenderink, 'Multiple Visual Worlds', *Perception*, 30 (2001), 1–7.
3. Theo van Leeuwen, *The Language of Color – An Introduction* (London: Routledge, Taylor and Francis Group, 2011), p. 74.
4. Katy Lithgow, Stavroula Golfomitsou and Catherine Dillon, 'Coming Clean about Cleaning. Professional and Public Perspectives: Are Conservators Truthful and Visitors Useful in Decision-Making?', *Studies in Conservation*, 63.S1 (2018), S392–S396.
5. W. Wei, I. Joosten, K. Keim, H. Douna, W. Mekking, M. Reuss and J. Wagemakers, 'Experience with Dust Measurements in Three Dutch Museums', *ZKK – Zeitschrift für Kunsttechnologie und Konservierung*, 21.2 (2007), 261–269.
6. Patrick Sandoz, Gilbert Tribillon, Tijani Gharbi and Robert Devillers, 'Roughness Measurement by Confocal Microscopy for Brightness Characterization and Surface Waviness Visibility Evaluation', *Wear*, 201 (1996), 186–192.
7. David Lange, Hamlin Jennings and Surendra Shah, 'Analysis of Surface Roughness Using Confocal Microscopy', *Journal of Materials Science*, 28 (1993), 3879–3884.
8. Amy E. Marquardt, Eric M. Breitung, Terry Drayman-Weisser, Glenn Gates and Raymond J. Phaneuf, 'Protecting Silver Cultural Heritage Objects with Atomic Layer Deposited Corrosion Barriers', *Heritage Science*, 3 (2015), Article number 37.
9. Marianna Barberio, Simona Veltri, Fabio Stranges, Assunta Bonanno, Fang Xu and Patrizio Antici, 'AFM and Pulsed Laser Ablation Methods for Cultural Heritage: Application to Archeometric Analysis of Stone Artifacts', *Applied Physics A*, 120 (2015), 909–916.
10. Tom Malzbender, Dan Gelb and Hans Wolters, 'Polynomial Texture Maps', *Proceedings of ACM SIGGRAPH Computer Graphics* (August 2001), 519–528. <https://doi.org/10.1145/383259.383320>
11. Emma Marie Payne, 'Imaging Techniques in Conservation', *Journal of Conservation and Museum Studies*, 10.2 (2012), 17–29.
12. Klaus Pollmeier and Jonathan Arney, 'Edge Reflection Analysis: A New Technique for the Documentation and Characterization of Photographic and Other Glossy Surfaces', *Studies in Conservation*, 47.S3 (2002), 160–164.
13. Jan Koenderink, 'Trieste in the Mirror', *Perception*, 29.2 (2000), 127-133.
14. Paul-Bernhard Eipper, 'Die Überprüfung von mit Tensiden gereinigten Oberlfächen durch die computergestützte Laser-Profilometries', in *Vier Künstlerfarbenhersteller zwischen 1900 und 1970: Die Reinigung von Gemäldeoberflächen mit wässrigen Systemen* (Bern: Verlag Paul Haupt, 1997), Section II.3, pp. 36–67.
15. William Wei, 'Surface Micro-Roughness, Cleaning and Perception', in *Proceedings of the ICOM-CC 16th Triennial Meeting*, September 19–23, Lisbon (Paris: International Council of Museums, 2011), Paper 1617.
16. Maartje Stoop, 'Investigating Protective Coatings for PVSc Wall Painting Detachment by Strappo' (APPII master's thesis, University of Amsterdam, 2019).
17. William Wei, 'International Research on the Conservation and Restoration of Face-Mounted Photographs', in *Proceedings of the ICOM-CC 15th Triennial Meeting*, September 22–26, New Delhi, Vol. 1, ed. by Janet Bridgland (Paris: International Congress of Museums, 2008), pp. 709–715.

18. W. (Bill) Wei, *Unpublished Results* (Cultural Heritage Agency of the Netherlands, 2011).

19. Paul Messier, Richard Johnson, Henry Wilhelm, Willam A. Sethares, Andrew Klein, Patrice Abry, Stephane Jaffard, Herwig Wendt, Stéphane Roux, Nelly Pustelnik, Nanne van Noord, Laurens van der Maaten and Eric Postma, 'Automated Surface Texture Classification of Inkjet and Photographic Media', in *Proceedings of NIP 29: International Conference on Digital Printing Technologies*, September 29 – October 3, 2013, Seattle (Springfield: Society for Imaging Sciences and Technology, 2013), pp. 85–91.

20. Paul Messier, 'Image Isn't Everything: Revealing Affinities across Collections Through the Language of the Photographic Print', in *Object: Photo. Modern Photographs: The Thomas Walther Collection 1909–1949*, ed. by Mitra Abbaspour, Lee Ann Daffner and Maria Morris Hambourg (New York: The Museum of Modern Art, 2014). <www.moma.org/interactives/objectphoto/assets/essays/Messier.pdf> [accessed 13 January 2023].

21. W. (Bill) Wei and Sanneke Stigter, 'Surface Roughness, Appearance, and Identification of AGFA-Gevaert Photograph Samples', in *Topics in Photographic Preservation*, Vol. 17, Photograph Materials Group of the AIC (Washington, DC: American Institute for Conservation, 2017), pp. 11–24.

22. W. (Bill) Wei, *Unpublished Results* (Cultural Heritage Agency of the Netherlands, 2006).

23. David Ford and Stuart Adams, 'Deposition Rates of Particulate Matter in the Internal Environment of Two London Museums', *Atmospheric Environment*, 33 (1999), 4901-4907.

24. Stuart J. Adams, Richard Kibrya and Peter Brimblecombe, 'A Particle Accumulation Study during the Reconstruction of the Great Court, British Museum', *Journal of Cultural Heritage*, 3 (2002), 283–287.

5 Digitization and reproduction technology

In Chapters 3 and 4, innovations in color science and roughness measurements were briefly reviewed and juxtaposed with current thinking on human perception. It was shown that innovations in color science and high-resolution digital imaging have provided capabilities for examining works of art down to the miniscule level of pigment particles, for nondestructive analysis of paint materials, and for improved documentation of objects. However, it was questioned what the use of so-called high resolution is if the humans cannot even see and perceive that resolution. Further, it was shown that images produced by high-resolution imaging systems still do not look real. What is missing in current digital images of objects, especially two-dimensional objects such as paintings and photographs, is the effect of surface texture and roughness. In Chapter 4, the role of roughness/texture in the appearance of works of art was discussed in more detail. It was shown that modern methods for measuring roughness and gloss can be used to help describe the effect of this "third dimension" of surfaces.

This chapter will now look at innovation trends in modern conservation science, revolving around the use of digital imaging technology, color science, and roughness to produce works of art which are as realistic as possible for research and for viewing. This chapter will revisit the discussions begun in Chapter 2, and look into what it is that the viewer is looking at when viewing a high-resolution digital image or reproduction, how such reproductions relate to the actual object and to its original or other appearance, and how the public perceives such images.

5.1 Rendering

The art of trying to make objects, scenery, and living beings look real is known as rendering. Many works of art are actually examples of rendering. However, in modern-day terms, results of the technology of rendering are perhaps most familiar to readers who are modern movie fans. Applications include making humans do stunts which are impossible even for the best of stuntpersons, making androids look real or aliens look "life-like," having cartoon and

DOI: 10.4324/9781003217800-5

animal figures carry out human actions, and creating fantasy scenery which is somehow believable to human viewers.

As described in Section 3.1, the production of "high-quality," "high-resolution," "true color" digital images of works of art is now possible by techniques which also fall under the term rendering. Multi- and hyperspectral imaging were shown to provide reflectance spectra for every pixel of a digital image. With those results, the color scientist or color expert can calculate the CIELAB colors and have them digitally printed using CMYK technology. While the use of digital technology and color science has pretty much matured, witness the many guides to graphic design (e.g., [1]), making something look real in terms of lighting, shadowing, reflection, and/or gloss continues to be a challenge for graphic film professionals. The scattering of light from a rough surface is far more complex than the simple description that was given for gloss in Section 4.2, Fig. 4.3. One needs to properly model light scattering in all directions from a surface. Classical artists have solved this problem with the combination of paint, glazes, and texture, but the effects which they have successfully created on canvas are largely lost in a flat digital reproduction.

The scattering of light from surfaces including varnishes can be mathematically modeled using so-called bi-directional reflection distribution functions (BRDFs) (see, e.g., [2–4]), and by experimentally studying how viewers see geometric shapes (see, e.g., [5, 6]). Such mathematical functions have been used, for example, for studies on how viewers see three-dimensional sculptures and how they then can be properly rendered. However, a number of problems come up when trying to move on to rendering humans and other three-dimensional scenes.

One of the main problems is describing the roughness of the surface from which the scattering is to be modeled. As was discussed in Section 4.3, it is certainly possible to measure roughness down to tens of nanometers resolution. Using this information in a BRDF mode is, however, an expensive computer modeling proposition. There are libraries of artificially produced texture maps available, but these are only an approximation of the real surface roughness of objects which vary locally.

A further problem with rendering objects is reproducing the effects of lighting. Many advances have been made in studying lighting effects on works of art, including the use of raking light and more recently the PTM technique described in Section 4.4. However, such techniques only use a specific source of lighting. If one is trying to render an object or space in a real context, multiple reflections of light from any surface near the object will also play a role in its final appearance (see, e.g., [7]). The reader may already be subconsciously aware of this when looking at, for example, an artist's rendition of plans for home interiors or new housing, and also when visualizing historic interiors. While perhaps useful to give an indication of original appearance, the actual appearance of the renderings lies somewhere between a drawing or cartoon, and reality (see, e.g., [8, 9]). This is because truly realistic rendering with multiple scattering is quite (computer) time-consuming and costly, and not necessary for many such applications.

The problem of rendering the effect of lighting is apparent in visualizations of historic interiors which are supposed to give the public an idea of what the place originally looked like. But what many of the models fail to account for is the ever-changing natural lighting, which was originally used (see, e.g., a discussion of light and color in the Throne Room in the Palace of Knossos by K. Soar [10]). Soar notes:

> The use of natural light, either sunlight or moonlight via windows, doorways and partitions of firelight, would emphasize specific aspects of these paintings, suggesting that the experience of viewing them would not have been a static activity, but one that was temporally mutable.
>
> [10]

Ivanovici also considers the role of time in a viewer's gaze as differentiated with momentary sight:

> In dealing with the luminous dimension of Late Antique churches one thus needs to consider both sight and gaze, adding the luminous valence of the textures and hues to the hierarchy of volumes and the increasing amount of natural and artificial light. The recognition of the perception of these details in luminous key enriches our understanding of the spaces' design, revealing the care taken by bishops in creating a luminous sequence.
>
> [11]

A special problem is that associated with rendering humans. Human skin is a translucent surface including oily films, hairs, skin surface, and subsurface layers. For digital rendering, it is necessary to model the reflection of light, not only from the inhomogeneous structure of the surface of skin, but also from the inhomogeneous distribution of hairs and oil, and, furthermore, accounting for the fact that skin is translucent, thus accounting for subsurface effects (see, e.g., early work by Pont and Koenderink [12]).

The cartoon effect mentioned above is also evident in the problem of the rendering of shadows. Most renderings that one comes across have a sharp delineation between lighted areas and shadowed areas. Real shadows have unsharp edges due to diffraction effects at the borders of the objects.

And then there is the question which continues to be posed in this book, as to how precise rendering of a work of art must be. In the beginnings of modern filmmaking, filmmakers of movies with fantasy figures worked with models which were painstakingly moved bit by bit, filmed frame by frame, so that when the film was shown at speed, one had the impression that the figure was moving. Those who have seen old Japanese monster movies from the 1950s and 1960s will understand the moment when this author, as a young boy, no longer became scared of the monsters when he learned about this technique and realized how jerky the monsters' movements actually were. As rendering improved, scenes became more realistic and scarier. However, at some point, the film industry noted that it was no longer necessary to strive for perfect rendering, because real actors or rendered living beings are moving and scenes change fairly quickly. A relatively good-quality rendering is thus sufficient because the viewer is too engrossed in the story line and the action to really notice that, for example, an android is not real.

This is, of course, not the case for a rendered work of art which sits still on a computer screen or high-quality print. The question still remains as to how high the color resolution must be for a "realistic" appearance. As discussed in Section 3.2, the question is whether viewers can really see the millions of pixels of color that are produced in a rendered, "true-color" digital image. On the other hand, viewers are certainly missing something important if they cannot perceive the effects of texture due to impasto or tell the difference between an oil painting and a pastel painting as mentioned in Section 4.1.

This question of texture also comes up for other historic objects of historic value but which do not receive as much media attention such as textiles. Lennard et al. [13] conducted research on the issues of matching color in the conservation of textiles with disturbing lacunae. They found that traditional methods of using other materials to neutrally fill missing pieces ran into problems due to the difference in physical and mechanical properties with the original materials, and matching the texture of the textiles. Photoshop™ and digital printing techniques were used to try to match color, this being a more economically attractive method than trying to make a large number of dye samples. However, it was also found that printed simulated texture was also needed. The ultimate choice of fill still depended on the surface texture of the object and the conservator/public eye. Printed textures would allow for a good blend for the viewer when viewing the object at normal viewing distance, but be obvious close up.

5.2   Digital reproductions of works of art

The issue of "true" color and texture is most evident in the digital reproduction of works of art, whether two- or three-dimensional. Every day, during the summer months, one sees hordes of tourists in the museum shops of major art museums buying posters of one of the famous paintings which they had just seen, or at least took a selfie of themselves standing next to it. These used to be produced using analogue color photographs of the painting under "ideal" lighting conditions.

Similar developments have occurred in the printing industry. The advent of analogue color photography and printing techniques allowed the production of "full color" versions of the art books, catalogues, coffee table books, and popular artist series mentioned at the beginning of Section 2.2. With time, the prints in these books tend to age, generally getting darker as one can often see in used copies available at almost any secondhand store. They are now being replaced with catalogues containing glossy, high-quality, "true-color" digitally printed photographs, with the expensive versions again originating from hyperspectral imaging systems. Furthermore, tourists can now pay a little more to obtain a framed, "true-color" high-resolution print.

Whether the buyer will notice the difference in the print after a few weeks, months, or years hanging on a wall in their homes is open to question. When they first purchase the print, there is an initial moment that the print seems to be of great value, the first value moment. But after hanging for a long time, it becomes part of the background, the second value moment, unless someone points it out, or it is damaged or lost, the third value moment. This is equivalent to issues in the conservation of outdoor sculpture, where there is a first value moment when a sculpture is placed, and the neighborhood has all sorts of opinions about it, from positive to negative [14]. This is followed by periods of time up to years when no one even notices it anymore, until the moment that someone points it out or even tries to do something with it.

If one considers texture as discussed in Chapter 4, it has become possible for tourists to spend even more money to buy a digital print of the painting on canvas making it appear as if has texture. The ultimate souvenir is now a high-quality copy of a painting hand-painted in China. The lucky buyer has something that looks like the original they saw in the museum.

However, consider the purchase the other way around. There are countless numbers of people who will most likely never be able to see an original Monet or Rembrandt or Rodin. To decorate their homes or to be able to study these works, they also buy high-quality digital reproductions of these works as framed posters or glossy coffee-table tomes. What is it that they are looking at? And what happens if, one day, they actually do get lucky enough to see one of the works of art in person?

To serve this public who may never be able to visit a major international museum, museums also make use of high-resolution digital images of works of art for display on the internet in so-called virtual museums, or by placing a complete digital archive of their collection online. There are examples where the public can view paintings down to the miniscule level of single cracks in the craquelure or of pigment particles. The question is why? While it is fascinating, the general museum public generally does not look at real paintings in that detail, partly because they don't have the equipment to do that, partly because they tend more to look at pictures as a whole, and partly because the guards would be called if they got that close. Furthermore, as discussed previously, the objects (paintings) are flat color reproductions on a computer screen. The entire experience of the texture of the painting is missing.

On a similar line of thought, it is noted that there has been increasing interest in the heritage world for using digital reproductions in virtual or augmented reality (see, e.g., [15, 16]). Viewers wear special goggles so that they are either entirely situated in a virtual representation of, for example, a historic building (VR – virtual reality), or they see a virtual reproduction of an object exhibited in, for example, a museum, but still see the actual surroundings of the exhibition room in which the virtual object is placed (AR – augmented reality). Furthermore, there has been increased interest in the production of replicas of three-dimensional objects. The replicas can be used to provide museum visitors with a chance to physically interact with objects without damaging the original. Physical replicas or digital replicas in VR and AR can also act as a substitute for an extremely fragile object which cannot be exhibited for extended periods. Again, while such replicas can be produced in "true color," the entire physical feel of the object is missing in VR and AR, and only approximated for a physical replica, not to speak of the lack of context. And what is it that one has seen?

It is now common that when people actually go to a museum and see an object, in particular a famous one, they exclaim, "I saw this in my art history book!" something which the author has also done. What is then the original? The actual work or the reproduction on the internet or in the art history book? A case in point discussed by Bruno Latour was the "return" of Veronese's *Wedding at Cana* to the refectory of the monastery in Venice [17]. The painting had been taken by Napoleon's army to Paris, and now hangs in the Louvre, across from a painting which is a bit more well-known, Leonardo da Vinci's "Mona Lisa." Requests for the return of the painting have long been rejected. However, permission was given to have it digitized and have a life-size high-resolution image made. In order to make it even more realistic, some of it was airbrushed to give it more the physical appearance of the painting. It is reported that older residents of the neighborhood cried when "their" Veronesi came back.

5.3   Virtual retouching

The innovations and advances in digital imaging and color science have also been the motivation to renew efforts to fulfill the wish to be able to see an object in its original condition as it leaves the artist's studio. Given the ethical need to minimalize the amount of retouching one does on a work of art and, if that is to be done, to avoid too much testing, conservators are now turning to the technique of "virtual retouching," or, in everyday terminology, "Photoshopping," named after the well-known software from Adobe Inc. Virtual retouching research has focused on two main objectives:

- testing methods for retouching paintings and polychrome objects including filling in lacunae
- trying to recover the original color of an object.

Early mention of virtual retouching was the addition of a missing 12 cm from Vermeer's *"Christ in the House of Mary and Martha,* using what was then called a "digital medium" [18]. Examples of the use of color processing technology and hyperspectral imaging for the virtual restoration of Chinese paintings and calligraphy are discussed [19, 20]. The filling in of relatively large lacunae in paintings by Martin and Van Gogh was discussed in relation to eye-tracking in Section 2.3. The author has also applied virtual retouching to assist conservators with visualizing the infilling of the damaged lower left-hand corner of Van Gogh's painting *Sea at Scheveningen* (1882) [21] and understanding the green area under the chair in one of the versions of his painting *The Bedroom* (1888) [22]. It is important to note that in all cases, while the persons doing the virtual retouch were making use of high-resolution color imaging and processing technology, they were still producing something based on their own subjective opinions.

Another innovative application of color science is the correction of faded works of art or the filling of lacunae using projections of corrections onto the object itself. Such projections have the advantage that they can make use of the roughness of the object itself. One of the first such attempts to restore an object with projected color was made by S. Stigter [23]. A number of colored filters were used to correct discoloration of the photographic components of a mixed media object, "Roquebrune" (1979), by the Dutch artist, Ger van Elk. These filters were chosen by experimentation. A green filter was used to neutralize the magenta discoloration of the photograph, and a straw-colored filter was used to try to bring back the original brownish tint. This lighting work was performed on a flat surface of a three-dimensional object. The work was conducted while the artist was alive, so that the final result could be properly judged before exhibition.

A group led by Daniel Aliaga at Purdue University used projections of infills designed by an art historian to virtually retouch three-dimensional objects including Chinese vases and American Indian pottery [24, 25]. This type of work looked for solutions for projecting corrections in a geometrically correct manner. However, at the time, color gradients were difficult to handle with the software used, which is, however, now possible with current commercially available software. At the Natural History Museum in Paris, Viénot and others [26] used LED light projections to try to bring back the original color of bird specimens. It was noted that observer testing was required to judge the appearance of the virtually retouched birds. It is interesting to note that the actual reversible recoloring of bird specimens recently conducted at the University of Pennsylvania museum also required considerable trial and error to find the right materials and pigments to bring back the original colors of faded feathers [27, 28].

A more widely publicized projection of a virtual retouch was the color correction of Mark Rothko paintings at the Museum of Fine Arts in Boston. This project provides a good example of the use of advances in color science and technology to attempt to bring the original color of an object back [29]. The paintings were badly discolored, having hung for many years exposed to direct sunlight. In order to allow viewers to see what the paintings originally looked like, colored light was projected onto the paintings. The color of the projected light was a corrective color based on Ektachrome™ slides taken of the new paintings, whereby it is noted that the Ektachrome™ slides themselves were color-corrected, making the actual projection a double correction. The exhibition was considered a great success. However, it also elicited important questions about what one is looking at when looking at a virtually retouched painting [30]. For example, visitors were disturbed by the extra light reflected from an essentially monochrome painting, and by their own shadows cast on the works as they stood before them. They were also disturbed by the concept of looking at the discolored original and the restored version at the same time.

5.4   Digital reproductions and light

In Section 5.1, the problem of rendering the effects of natural and artificial lighting was introduced. The issue of extra reflected light just mentioned is, however, a different problem. Unlike contemporary works of art which actually use sources of light, or transparent or translucent objects such as stained glass or three-dimensional glass objects, opaque objects require that light be shone on them in order for them to be seen. Depending on their "color," they will produce their own light in the sense that the viewer will perceive them to be brighter or darker. Barnett Newman, for example, wanted viewers to stand close to his monochrome works so that they would be surrounded by the color [31]. But that is totally different than the Rothko virtual retouching case, where the color is projected onto the painting and then reflected back to the viewer. One may be able to see an "original" color, but the perception is different than if one had been standing in front of the painting "producing its own light" when it first left the easel.

This issue also plays a role in how to handle a local retouch such as that performed on Van Gogh's *An Old Woman of Arles*, discussed in Section 2.3. Two issues of perception come up besides the fact that even professionals did not notice that the lacuna that was being retouched was located at the lower left-hand corner of a portrait. The first issue is the fact that the choice of neutral color for infilling was originally the "standard" answer of a neutral gray. However, it was subjectively found that a blue green which combined the blues and greens in the woman's cloak was actually less obvious. A second issue which came up was how to project such a correction onto the painting for exhibition purposes. In experiments with a "true color" poster of the painting, it was found that in order to make the projection of the realistic retouch blend into the painting, the lighting of the rest of the painting had to match the brightness of the retouch in order to avoid having a "glow glob" in the lower left-hand corner [32]. While it is fairly simple to calculate what that brightness must be, it ultimately comes down to the decision of the exhibition curator as to what the lighting should be, as well as the consideration that this would be a higher-intensity lighting than what the painting would normally receive. Otherwise, the virtual retouch would not stand out above the gray retouch it was meant to cover up.

Another problem with virtual reproductions and light are the popular projections of "original colors" on tapestries and wall paintings in historic buildings. There are numerous examples of such techniques being developed to provide the viewer with an idea of what a faded or missing interior or tapestry looked like originally based on digital (hyperspectral) color imaging (see, e.g., [33, 34]). In the case of the tapestry, color projection was designed based on studies of the colors found on the backside, which would not have discolored as much as the front through the ages. It is perhaps a matter of taste if one likes to look at a bright "true-color" projection which always has a cartoony impression. However, the image shown on the internet does not do justice to what one would feel if one had been standing in front of the real object and project (which this author had not). One could question what it was that the viewer saw. The claim, of course, would be that one would have an idea of how the tapestry originally appeared. But human memory does not remember that piece of information. Rather, what remains is an image of a tapestry which glows with colors that are applied transparently to the canvas.

5.5   The dark side

In this chapter, the use of innovations in color science and texture measurements for innovations in digital reproductions and virtual retouching have been discussed. Many of the advantages of these techniques have been highlighted, but the question of what one is seeing as compared to the original object has also been posed a number of times. Possible answers to these questions will be presented in the following chapter. However, before going into that discussion, this chapter ends with the note that there will unfortunately always be a few who find a way to misuse what were innovations with good intentions.

It has been shown that color science and digital technology can reproduce works of art in true color. While the lack of texture prevents such reproductions from really looking real, it was also shown that the roughness/texture of surfaces can be measured to submicron levels using commercially available profilometers, and almost to atomic levels using instruments such as atomic force microscopy which was discussed at the end of Section 4.3. The production of high-quality copies of paintings in China is also well known.

Consider now for a moment a number of other significant areas of industrial research and development, that of thin films and coatings, and that of rapid prototyping. The computer industry has long been capable of producing computer chips by depositing atomic layers of gold, silicon, silicon dioxide, and other metals and metalloids in complex patterns. It is also possible to deposit atomic layers of materials for corrosion protection, protection against wear, as reflective coatings, and for decorative purposes.

At a somewhat larger scale, rapid prototyping makes use of certain types of plastics to build up prototypes of products layer by layer (see, e.g., [35]). Wall thicknesses of 10s of micrometers are possible, and research is continuing to reduce that value or, in other words, increase the resolution with which one can make 3D objects. The production of works of art using rapid prototyping technology is becoming popular among artists [36–38], and, as noted in Section 5.2, museums are making more use of replicas in their exhibitions.

Given the rapid advances in technology in the past decades, it is not unimaginable that at some point in the near future, increasingly better copies of works of arts will start appearing on the market, with true color at pixel level, the proper chemistry, and the exact surface roughness of the entire original object. A roughness measurement, such as that described in Section 4.3, can be made on a work of art at a particular position known only to the owner and the institute performing the measurements. This can be used as a "fingerprint" of the object. This does not prevent its theft, but if there is a database of object "passports" including provenance records and the fingerprint, it does make it much more difficult for thieves to resell the object [39, 40]. However, profilometry can conceivably be used to measure the microroughness of an entire work. This information can be fed into a CAD (computer-aided design) file which then can be used to steer a rapid prototyping machine to exactly reproduce the surface texture of the work. Add the "true color" and, voila, one has an exact copy of the work, indistinguishable from the original except at a chemical level, assuming that the forger does not also use recipes for the original materials, which are then artificially aged. Totally unrealistic, a pipe-dream, many readers will say. It will only be noted that highly skilled forgers are still fooling museums and art collectors today and looking for more ways to do that. Given the prices being paid for art these days, the costs of making an almost exact copy using the technologies described in the previous chapters are not as exorbitant as one would think.

5.6   Summary of Chapter 5

In this chapter, the combination of the tools of color science, roughness measurements, and digital imaging was discussed in terms of the technology of rendering, that is, reproducing works of art as realistic as possible. The objective of innovative efforts in color science, digital technology, and surface roughness measurements is to reproduce a work of art as realistic, which is the concept of rendering. Rendering is common in filmmaking, where rendered subjects are on the move so that the viewer does not notice their imperfections. Rendering of motionless works of art is much more difficult. Besides the question of whether the colors which are used are true, modeling texture and lighting effects requires an immense amount of computational effort, and the results still appear cartoon-like to various degrees. Projecting corrections onto a work of art supposedly provides an indication of how it used to appear. The question is, however, what one is looking at, especially since the projection reflects back unnaturally to the viewer. Rendering in the form of virtual retouching is, however, a useful tool to give conservators an indication of what a treatment might look like. Even if it were possible to render an object perfectly, the danger is that, given the value of many works of art, exact copies of works can be made.

References

1. John T. Drew and Sara A. Meyer, *Color Management – A Comprehensive Guide for Graphic Designers* (Mies: RotoVision SA, 2008).
2. Gregory J. Ward, 'Measuring and Modeling Anisotropic Reflection', *Computer Graphics*, 26.2 (1992), 265–272.
3. Mady Elias and Lionel Simonot, 'Bi-Directional Reflectance of a Varnished Painting Part I: Influence of the Refractive Indices without Using the Approximations of Saunderson Correction – Exact Computation', *Optics Communications*, 231 (2004), 17–24.
4. Mady Elias, Lionel Simonot, Mathieu Thoury and Jean Marc Frigerio, 'Bi-Directional Reflectance of a Varnished Painting Part II: Comparison between the Effects of the Refractive Indices, of the Surface States and of the Absorption of the Varnish – Experiments and Simulations', *Optics Communications*, 231 (2004), 25–33.
5. Jan J. Koenderink, Andrea J. van Doorn and Joseph S. Lappin, 'Direct Measurement of the Curvature of Visual Space', *Perception*, 29 (2000), 69–79.
6. Jan Koenderink, Andrea van Doorn and Johan Wagemans, 'Part and Whole in Pictorial Relief', *i-Perception*, 6.6 (2015), 1–21.
7. Simon Premože, Michael Ashikhmin, Ravi Ramamoorthi and Shree Nayar, 'Practical Rendering of Multiple Scattering Effects in Participating Media', in *Proceedings of the 15th Eurographics Workshop on Rendering* Techniques, June 21–23, Norköping, ed. by H. W. Jensen, Alexander Keller and Henrik Jensen (Eindhoven: The Eurographics Association, 2004).
8. Lucía Perira-Pardo, Diego Tamburini and Joanne Dyer, 'Shedding Light on the Colours of Medieval Alabaster Sculptures: Scientific Analysis and Digital Reconstruction of Their Original Polychromy', *Color Research & Application*, 44.2 (2018), 221–233.
9. *Kleur! bij Grieken en Etrusken* (Color of the Greeks and Etruscans), in Dutch, ed. By Hrman Brijder, Gerala Jurriaans and Marion Mosler (Zwolle: Wanders Uitgevers, 2005).
10. Katy Soar, 'By the Dawn's Early Light: Color Light and Liminality in the Throne Room at Knossos', in *Color and Light in Ancient and Medieval Art*, ed. by Chloë N. Duckworth and Anne E. Sassin (London: Routledge, 2018), p. 46.
11. Vladimir Ivanovici, 'Divine Light Through Earthly Colors: Mediating Perception in Late Antique Churches', in *Color and Light in Ancient and Medieval Art*, ed. by Chloë N. Duckworth and Anne E. Sassin (London: Routledge, 2018), p. 85.

12. J. Koenderink and S. Pont, '"The Secret of Velvety Skin"', in Machine Vision and Applications – Special Issue on Human Modeling', *Analysis and Synthesis*, 14 (2003), 260–268.

13. Frances Lennard, Thórdis Baldursdóttir and Vicky Loosemore, 'Using Digital and Hand Printing Techniques to Compensate for Loss: Re-Establishing Color and Texture in Historic Textiles', *The Conservator*, 31.1 (2008), 55–65.

14. W. (Bill) Wei, Hanneke Heerema, Rebecca Rushfeld and Ida van der Lee, 'Issues in Conservation – Three Value Moments in the Public Perception of Cultural Heritage Objects in Public Spaces', *Collabra: Psychology* (2021). <https://doi.org/10.1525/collabra.21935>

15. Rafaá Wojciechowsk, Krzysztof Walczak, Martin White and Wojciech Cellary, 'Building Virtual and Augmented Reality Museum Exhibitions', in *Proceedings of the Ninth International Conference on 3D Web Technology*, Web3D 2004, April 5–8, Monterey (Chicago: SIGGRAPH, 2004), pp. 135–144 and 187.

16. Yuting Zhou, Juanjuan Chen and Minhong Wang, 'A Meta-Analytic Review on Incorporating Virtual and Augmented Reality in Museum Learning', *Education Research Review*, 26 (2022). <https://doi.org/10.1016/j.edurev.2022.100454>

17. Bruno Latour, 'The Migration of the Aura, or How to Explore the Original Through Its Facsimiles', in *Switching Codes: Thinking Through Digital Technology in the Humanities and the Arts*, ed. by Thomas Bartscherer and Roderick Coover (Chicago: University of Chicago Press, 2004), pp. 205–229.

18. Jørgen Wadum, 'Ravished Images Restored', in *Personal Viewpoints: Thoughts About Paintings Conservation*, ed. by Mark Leonard (Los Angeles: The Getty Conservation Institute, 2003), p. 66.

19. Soo-Chang Pei, Yi-Chong Zeng and Ching-Hua Chang, 'Virtual Restoration of Ancient Chinese Paintings Using Color Contrast Enhancement and Lacuna Texture Synthesis', *IEEE Transactions on Image Processing*, 13.3 (2004), 416–429.

20. Wu Wangting, Hou Miaole and Lv Shuqiang, 'Application of Hyperspectral Imaging Technology to the Analysis and Research of Chinese Paintings and Calligraphy', in *ICOM Committee for Conservation 19th Triennial Meeting Copenhagen Preprints*, ed. by Janet Bridgland (Paris: International Congress of Museums, 2021), paper no. 187.

21. W. (Bill) Wei, *Unpublished Research* (Cultural Heritage Agency of the Netherlands, 2018).

22. W. (Bill) Wei, *Unpublished Research* (Cultural Heritage Agency of the Netherlands, 2017).

23. Sanneke Stigter, 'Living Artist, Living Artwork? The Problem of Faded Color Photographs in the Work of Ger van Elk', *Studies in Conservation*, 49.suppl 2 (2004), 105–108.

24. Daniel G. Aliaga, Alvin J. Law and Yu Hong Yeung, 'A Virtual Restoration Stage for Real-World Objects', in *Proceedings ACM SIGGRAPH Asia, ACM Transactions on Graphics*, 27.5 (2008), 1–10.

25. Alvin J. Law, Daniel G. Aliaga, Yu Hong Yeung, Richard McCoy, Amy McKune and Larry Zimmerman, 'Projecting Restorations in Real-Time for Real-World Objects', in *Proceedings Museums and the Web 2009*, April 15–18, Indianapolis, ed. by Jennifer Trant and David Bearman (Toronto: Archives & Museum Informatics, 2009).

26. Françoise Viénot, Guillaume Coron and Bertrand Lavédrine, 'LEDs as a Tool to Enhance Faded Colours of Museums Artefacts', *Journal of Cultural Heritage*, 12.4 (2011), 431–440.

27. Julia, Sybalsky, Lisa Elkin, Michaela Paulson, Fran E. Ritchie and Click Nether-field, 'Restoring Color to Faded Feathers and Fur', in *Presentation at the American Institute of Conservation Annual Meeting*, May 18, 2013, Jacksonville.
28. Michaela Paulson, Private Communication (2023).
29. Santiago Cuellar, Jens Stenger, Rudolph Gschwind, Ankit Mohan, Yasuhiro Mukaigawa, Ramesh Raskar, Katherine Eremin and Narayan Khandekar, 'Non-Invasive Color Restoration of Faded Paintings Using Light from a Digital Projector', in *ICOM Committee for Conservation 16th Triennial Meeting Lisbon Preprints*, ed. by Janet Bridgland (Paris: International Congress of Museums, 2011), paper no. 749.
30. L. Menand, 'Watching Them Turn Off the Rothkos', *The New Yorker* (April 1, 2015). <https://www.newyorker.com/culture/cultural-comment/watching-them-turn-off-the-rothkos> [accessed 14 October 2023].
31. Magreeth Soeting, 'A Close Look at *Cathedra*', in *Barnett Newman: Cathedra*, ed. by Jan van Adrichem (Amsterdam: Stedelijk Museum, 2001), p. 31.
32. W. (Bill) Wei, *Unpublished Research* (Cultural Heritage Agency of the Nether-lands, 2017).
33. Massimo Limoncelli, *Virtual Restoration 1 – Paintings and Mosaics* (Rome: L'Erma di Bretschneider, 2017).
34. <www.manchester.ac.uk/discover/news/scientists-virtually-restore-16th-century-tapestry-at-hampton-court-palace/> [accessed 6 May 2023].
35. Eef Moeskopf and Frits Feenstra, 'Introduction to Rapid Prototyping', in *Reverse Engineering*, ed. by Vinesh Raja and Kiran Fernandes (London: Springer, 2008), chapter 5, pp. 99–117.
36. Michael Rees, 'Rapid Prototyping and Art', *Rapid Prototyping Journal*, 5.4 (1999), 154–167.
37. Stephen Hoskins, *3D Printing for Artists, Designers and Makers* (London: Bloomsbury Academic, 2013).
38. Carolien Coon, Boris Pretzel, Tom Lomax and Matija Strlič, 'Preserving Rapid Prototypes: A Review', *Heritage Science*, 4 (2016), article no. 40.
39. William Wei, Josef Frohn, Sophia Sotiropolou and Mark Weber, 'Experience with a New Non-Contact Fingerprinting Method for the Identification and Protection of Objects of Cultural Heritage against Theft and Illegal Trafficking', in *Proceedings of the CSSIM Conference 'Conservation Strategies for Saving Indoor Metals Collections, Satellite Conference – Legal Issues in the Conservation of Cultural Heritage*, February 25 – March 1, Cairo (Athens: Technological Educational Institute of Athens, 2007), pp. 217–222.
40. William Wei, Vera Bakker, Anna Lagana, Josef Frohn, Andreas Walther, Georg Wiora, Mark Weber, Simon Goodall, Kirk Martinez and Sophia Sotiropolou, 'A Semi-Automatic System for the Non-Contact 'Fingerprinting' of Objects of Art and Cultural Heritage', in *Proceedings of the ICOM-CC 15th Triennial Meeting*, September 22–26, New Delhi, Vol. 1, ed. by Janet Bridgland (Paris: International Congress of Museums, 2008), pp. 376–380.

6 The future – a new reality

In this book, the development of conservation science for art conservation and subsequent innovations has been examined based on the real and perceived needs of conservators and their codes of ethics. However, as was discussed in Chapter 1, the term innovation only means new. That many technological innovations in art conservation are good goes without saying, but that does not mean that all innovations are good, nor does it mean that it is good to continue using them or improving on them. In Chapters 2–5, specific innovations have been examined related to the concept of "original appearance." These include color science, surface properties, and digital rendering and reproduction. The technical reviews were juxtaposed with discussions about perception and what a viewer of a work of art sees and perceives using these technologies. In this chapter, the role and effect of the precision color and digital imaging technology on art conservation will first be critically examined in light of the vagaries and subjectivity of the concept of original appearance and of what viewers actually see and perceive in works of art. The discussion then briefly returns to technological innovations in other scientific fields in art conservation. Finally, the debate is opened as to where technological innovation in art conservation should be going, and, above all, what role it plays in answering the questions of what it is that heritage professionals are telling the public to preserve, for whom, and for how long.

Technological innovations have brought the art conservation profession a long way from practical experience and experimentation which took place before the cleaning controversy at the National Gallery in London. It has provided conservators and other cultural heritage professionals with a better understanding of the properties of the materials used in a work of art, their current condition, and, thus, a better basis for making complex conservation decisions as required by Western conservation codes of ethics. Innovations in chemical analysis have provided conservation scientists with the ability to identify the chemical and physical properties of an object and the materials it was made of down to the finest submicroscopic detail. New and optimized analysis techniques have helped make it possible to identify previously unidentifiable materials and artists' mixtures of materials. In combination

DOI: 10.4324/9781003217800-6

with these advances and innovations in chemical analysis technology, color science and digital imaging technologies have provided nondestructive methods for analyzing materials in works of art. They have also helped heritage professionals better understand the effects of lighting on what they see in terms of color and texture. Along with other graphics professions, improved tools have been developed for rendering objects on the computer screen or making digital reproductions. Finally, digital technology is providing people who do not have the wherewithal to physically visit museums, to virtually visit them. Virtual reproductions and virtual and augmented reality tools also allow viewers to virtually see what a work of art or a historic site may originally have looked like.

As discussed in Chapters 3–5, much of the innovative work conducted in terms of color science and original appearance has, in recent years, been conducted mostly with digital technologies and viewed on professionally color-calibrated computer screens. If the real object is not available to the viewer, what most cultural heritage professionals and the general public view can be found in books and prints with a wide range of paper and printing quality, or viewed on a wide spectrum of computer screens and digital display monitors from the smallest mobile telephones and notebooks to the largest digital screens, each with varying quality, depending on how much money the user wants to spend.

The final critical discussion in this book on technological innovation in art conservation now begins with the last-mentioned viewing medium, the computer screen and the internet. The reader may recall having been asked the following question: "What was one of the most influential modern and innovative developments of the 19th and 20th centuries to affect art history?" The answer is photography. There are still many art historians writing about objects based only on photographs and drawings they have seen in books, and in many of those books, like this current book on color, all of the printed illustrations are only in black and white.[1] Even recently, Stephanie Aulsebrook cited Hurcombe concerning metallic works of art which are less likely than paintings to be published in color,

> Several significant barriers hinder our understanding of the importance of color and light properties of metal objects in past societies. Color has often been one of the first elements eliminated to control printing costs, with the majority of published artefacts presented in black and white."
>
> [1]

Now, with high-resolution innovations in color science, a generation of heritage professionals and the general public are becoming accustomed to looking at works of art on a computer screen or as digital prints. The colors which they are seeing have been programmed for viewing on the computer screen using, for example, sRGB and Adobe RGB standards, and for printing using

CMYK standards. These standards are all related to the CIELAB research and development conducted in the 20th century and discussed in Section 3.1. A form of such standards familiar to conservators can be seen in the modern documentation of conservation treatments, where standard color charts are always included in photographs of the objects to ensure that, even if the image changes with time, the known reference will also change in the same way as the rest of the image.

But what do such standards do beyond identifying colors as a set of numbers? Heritage professionals and the general viewing public want to see the "real" thing in an image, and, as discussed previously, much of innovation work has gone into producing digital images with "real" original colors. In terms of color, this is what Van Leeuwen calls color naturalism, based on the naturalistic truth of visual communication.

> In the case of naturalistic modality, the truth criterion is perceptual. It rests on the idea that the more a visual representation resembles what we would see if we saw the represented things in reality the truer people will think it is.
>
> [2]

He notes further, "For the moment it is important to note that, from the Renaissance on, naturalistic modality became the dominant truth criterion in visual representation. And to some degree, it still is, even in new media such as computer games."

As was noted earlier, there is no CIELAB standard observer, and there are significant differences in color perception and color language use between men and women, adults and children, and across cultures. Many discussions and debates about color will continue no matter what color resolution will be attained in the future. Humans with excellent vision can see up to roughly 10 million colors, but high-resolution systems can produce even more, more than billions or trillions in so-called 24- to 48-bit color depth.

How accurate the digital content is, is, however, dependent on the equipment used to image the object and the skill and expertise of the operator. Berns writes:

> The choice of camera is extremely important. The inherent limitations in spectral sensitivity and the differences between the reference and camera-taking light are mitigated to some extent through color management. When a camera is 'profiled', a reference target containing dozens or hundreds of color patches is imaged. Visual assessment, although very effect for qualitative evaluation, lacks precision for quantitative evaluation. Because of mismatches in viewing conditions (the display is often dimmer than the illuminated painting) differences in image size, the need to look back and forth between the painting and the display and the tendency for preferred

color reproduction, . . . A well-profiled or well-calibrated printer does not guarantee excellent results [3].

Whatever "excellent results" means, Berns later writes, "Achieving a high-quality reproduction or image archive is difficult. No matter who is doing the work and what their level of experience, there are fundamental limitations preventing perfection, which in any case remains to be defined."

If that is the case, the question is again as follows: what is being produced with "innovative" digital technology? Colantoni et al. [4] write in the introduction to their paper on multispectral imaging, for example,

> In fact, very high-definition digital images contain more details than the artist would have been able to see. In addition, with a dynamic range of 16-bit, the color accuracy contains more color levels than the human eye is able to identify. The digital content is more accurate than what the artist would have been able to perceive themselves and can give subtle information on the painter's technique.
>
> [4]

Are the works of art shown in true colors on a computer screen or a print then really the same as the real object? And what is the use of such color resolution if the human eye cannot see the difference?

Taking a further look at the question of lighting as touched upon in Sections 5.3 and 5.4 the reader is invited to think about how a work of art is seen in real life. With the exception of translucent or transparent works such as stained-glass windows or glass objects and contemporary works of art with light as part of the work, the lighting of a work of art is external to the work. How it appears depends on whether it is naturally or artificially lighted, if the light source is a spotlight or diffuse light, the angle with which the light is projected onto the work, and what color the light is and its intensity. The image of a work of art on a computer is, however, lighted by the screen; the work essentially lights itself. Although the lighting for glass objects also comes from behind the object, they have as a source of light something at a distance from the object, not as direct as a computer screen. Whether it is a truly bright and colorful work of art or a 17th-century masterpiece, they all come out bright and colorful. The noted Dutch architect Rem Koolhaas notes, as quoted by Van Leeuwen,

> We have increasingly been exposed to luminous color, as the virtual rapidly invaded our conscious experience – colour on TV, computers, movies – all potentially 'enhanced' and therefore more intense, more fantastic, more glamorous than any real color on real surface. Color, paint, coating, in comparison become matt and dull.
>
> [5]

Furthermore, as with images on a computer screen, it is a flat object with no texture. Contrary to what Berns wrote, a spectrally correct print will not appear as the painting appeared to a *plein air* artist.

When considering the precision with which colors are claimed to be reproduced, it is also important to consider the discussion of the unknown workings of human perception, and the vagaries of the philosophy of color discussed in Chapter 2 and Sections 3.2 and 3.3.

Recall from Section 2.1 that a digital (or analogue) print is lighted based on how the printer and color scientist calculate it should be and on colors determined by the so-called 2° CIELAB observer, not the way real individual people see and perceive. Furthermore, the precision of the language that those people do use to describe color and discuss the appearance, intent, and history of works of art, besides being culturally biased, does not come anywhere close to what color scientists claim to be reproducing. The descriptions do not include the original physical surroundings of the work and the original relationships between colors in a work, that is, the effects of contrast in harmony first described by Chevreul [6]. Recall also that it is becoming increasingly clear that the human perception system, in particular for the perception of color, does not at all work the way that color scientists assume.

So, what is the role of innovation in color and digital technology, what has it ultimately achieved, and where should it go? The answers to the first two questions have been discussed throughout this book. On the one hand, it has provided conservators with a nondestructive tool for analyzing works of (polychrome) art with less need for destructive chemical analysis. It has also provided more accurate tools for documenting their current appearance in a medium that is not subject to discoloration due to aging, assuming that the data can be read with future generations of computer software.

The answer as to where it should be going is a different story. It is difficult enough to understand a work when it hangs in the context of a museum rather than in the artist's studio or the residence or workplace of the work's first owner. Color scientists, technical art historians, and other heritage professionals continue to claim that these technologies have provided the means for people to see works of art in true color, and opens the possibilities for eventually determining their original appearance. And L. Tissen claims that virtual reproductions and 3D printing will allow visitors to engage with objects without physically interacting with the originals, developing new narratives [7].

However, the public around the world is now presented with bright, high-resolution color computer and print images of almost every work of art considered important on museum, art history, and gallery websites. They can purchase catalogues, specialty books, posters, and copies of objects online without ever having seen the real object. As, ironically, the color scientist Berns points out, "printed reproductions such as catalogues, books, and posters are usually viewed without the original painting available for comparison" [8]. So what color scientists, digital imaging specialists, and their heritage professionals have done is to produce a new reality of art, works which are manipulated to supposedly produce real colors, which are lighted from within themselves on the computer screen, or are as glossy as the paper upon which the reproductions are printed. High-resolution copies of three-dimensional works of art become the new reality of that art in the home. These reproduction images and models, and the new explanations and discoveries that accompany them, thus become the public's new reality of art and art history, but also of the student of art history in a far-off land with no access to the real object.

Is this innovation good? Going back fifteen years, Hans-Christoph von Imhoff wrote about art history and photography,

> I argue that, if this humanistic discipline, called history of art, continues to attribute, unravel, teach and explain art like it did in the last 100 years, i.e. by black and white photographs and later by mostly faded colour slides, it will continue to lose its credibility. I tried to demonstrate what the lack of physical perception and contact with panel- canvas-, wall – and whatever other paintings and the lack of knowledge of paintings' technicalities does do to the works and to the meaning of those works; and I very much fear that art historical research is taking the risk to fall off sound ground, unless it gets physically closer to the painting.
>
> [9]

Written not long ago, this complaint still applies, but now to the new reality of digital "true color" images.

For historians, lost are the discussions and debates face-to-face with the object, gone is the authenticity of the original (note that the words "authenticity" and "original" are used here as the dictionary meant them to be used), and gone is the feel for the role that the original/real object played when it was created and used (see the discussion in, e.g., [10]). Contrary to what color scientists claim, what the public sees and perceives of a work of art will look different than any computer image or high-resolution color print they may have at home. Every reader will have noticed this when going to a store to buy something that they thought was beautiful in a fashion magazine, or when visiting a house for sale which they saw beautifully photographed online. High-resolution reproductions are just not the same as the real object. And if one considers objects from other cultures which are considered to be art by Western collectors. as mentioned in Chapter 1.1, a reproduction does not do any justice to the real object in its original ritual context.

Unfortunately, honest assessments mentioned previously such as those by Berns about the limits of developments in color technology get snowed under the wealth of brilliant (in terms of brightness) online images provided by yet another "blockbuster" digital imaging project with a famous work of art, which claims to provide "true color" or perhaps even "original color" images with details such as microcracking at the highest possible spatial resolution, down to the micrometer level still discernable by the human eye. One can seriously ask what the objective of such "blockbuster" projects is besides great publicity for the museum and the funding agency. Besides using technology and personnel effort only affordable by the largest cultural heritage institutions, most museum visitors do not look at nor have a reason to look at objects in such detail.

Those fortunate and skilled enough to have the funding to perform such work claim that such documentation is in the interest of science and future restorations. However, from a materials engineering (fracture mechanics) standpoint, there is little point in observing craquelure in such detail in a properly climate-controlled museum. As industrial coating experts know, the crack pattern which one sees on centuries-old classic paintings and other polychrome objects will not extend any farther. The internal stresses in the paint layer (coating) have long since been released by the cracking itself. And measuring the depth of cracks using, for example, OCT (optical coherence tomography) [11] also serves no purpose in conservation since those cracks form instantly, and the problem with flaking and loss of paint is a horizontal one, that is, between the varnish or paint layer and the layer below it.

But in those examples on microcracking lies another rub to the acceptance of innovation in art conservation as "good." The science part of training programs in conservation and collection management focuses primarily on chemistry. This is understandable given that most conservation treatments and other measures are chemical in nature. This means that there is a serious lack of sufficient expertise in other science and engineering fields for conservation professionals and funding agencies to be able to make judgments about the value and applicability of innovations which they are constantly bombarded with. The claimed scientific need to document micro-cracking of centuries-old paintings is an example of a claim made with no background in the mechanical properties of materials.

Ultimately, funding applications for research are often successful for those scientists who can show spectacular innovative results and best prey on the fear of not having the proper information as required by conservation codes of ethics. One can, for example, ask why one needs to use an atomic force microscope to study corrosion phenomena that may take decades, if not centuries, to develop when museum climate controls are installed, instead of just a few years outdoors. For museum objects, the one or two atomic layers will not make any difference in their behavior under museum conditions, and normal conservation treatment intervals. Many mundane practical questions from smaller museums and private conservators that need to be answered are thus left by the wayside in the push for "innovative" research. The fact that most, if not all, conservation decisions are subject to varying degrees of interpretation and uncertainty, whether due to a lack of technical material evidence or a lack of historical information, which can be found using existing technologies, is all too often lost in funding requirements and the quest for newness and spectacular results. The question is then what these new technologies provide for the average conservator in the field. The claim by the richer museums and research institutes – that their research benefits them, a version of so-called trickle-down economics – just doesn't hold water.

In this author's opinion, there are many examples of so-called innovations in art conservation besides color science and digital imaging which, with some honest thought beforehand, need not have been developed or developed as far at the expense of other more useful practical research. The laser cleaning of works of art, for example, for removing varnish was publicized with much fanfare as being able to remove difficult varnish layers. People had already heard of micro-lasers and the wonders they could perform in medicine and semiconductor manufacturing. However, they forget the simple truth that a laser burns things, and that also quite violently on a microscale. Furthermore, it is also forgotten that lasers in the semiconductor industry are applied on very flat surfaces on an atomic scale. In early trials, conservator, K. Seymour, noted a number of issues with laser cleaning, including the fact that it cleans at one level, therefore leaving unwanted material in "valleys" [12]. It is also difficult for the detection system (LIBS – laser induced breakdown spectroscopy) to tell the difference between a repaint layer and an original oil paint layer, resulting in some damage of the original paint layer, and yellowing. In fact, the way the (automated) laser system knows that it has reached the paint layer is to begin measuring paint, but that is too late. Except for heavy cleaning of soot or the cleaning of outdoor objects which essentially are made of relatively large masses of substrate material such as stone, laser cleaning has not reached the level of application that had been hoped for by its developers.

Another example of an innovative technology that eventually bit the dust (pun intended) was the development of a video monitor for dust. The idea was that such a monitor could be placed at various locations in museums and detect dust in real time. A little thought and a literature study on dust management in industry and households would have shown that the results of the monitor would not be realistic, being very sensitive to what is happening locally right at the video monitor, but not to the long-term trends which actually are the problem. Experience shows [13] that dust monitoring only makes sense based on measurements taken at intervals of several weeks before there is a measurable change, and even then, some kind of perception testing is required to determine if the rate of dust accumulation is "bad."

On a different note, conservators often call for the measurement of dust on vertical surfaces, in addition to or rather than on horizontal surfaces, because that is the practical reality of dust collection on paintings. This is an example of the fear of not having collected enough information as required by codes of ethics and a concomitant lack of trust in risk analyses and statistics. Dust collects much faster on horizontal surfaces for hopefully obvious reasons. Most changes are visible within several months, allowing collection managers to adjust filter systems or cleaning intervals fairly rapidly. Monitoring on vertical surfaces would literally take years before one would obtain a sensible result. One can thus design anti-dust measures or cleaning intervals based on what happens with objects with horizontal surfaces, and the vertical surfaces will certainly be protected.

The search for the elusive original appearance of objects of art and cultural heritage will continue to fascinate professionals and the general public alike. Conservation scientists will thus continue to develop more advanced techniques to achieve these goals. For many, this will be done in the true belief that one can reach this elusive goal. Has scientific innovation really solved our problems of original appearance? To some extent, yes. But as Aulsebrook writes concerning the production of metal Bronze Age vessels,

> When scholars interact with metal artefacts firsthand they are lit under modern lights: constant, strong and a world away from the natural and artificial sources of sun and flame used in the past. . . . Their present condition becomes an aesthetic reflected back onto the past, creating a lens of distortion affecting interpretations: even ancient tools of violent warfare are rendered unthreatening due to their perceived fragility and pretty green coloration.
>
> [1]

Bernárdez-Vilaboa clearly states what one would think would be obvious, that "Any subjective evaluation procedure for a work of art can be affected by lighting and the living eye" [14].

There are, thus, limits as to how far such research can go, and, as discussed in this book, those limits are primarily determined by the limits set by the subjectivity of conservation decisions and art historical interpretation, and by the perception of the viewer. There should be more thoughtful consideration of what it is that conservation scientists with their advanced equipment are offering, and how this is related to daily conservation practice.

It would, for example, be more useful to use innovative technologies such as eye-tracking for perception testing with accompanying surveys and public discussion to determine what the public looks at, and then decide what is worth conserving and how to do that. One hears the screams and moans of strict interpreters of conservation codes of ethics, art historians, and other heritage professionals saying that the public has no idea what is valuable. That is the reason that so many conservators and heritage professionals are seen as an elite group, in spite of their weak protests to the contrary. It is, however, interesting to note the admission by J. Wadum about research interest in a painting thought to have been painted by Rubens, but then turned out not to be. "Naturally, the painting's status declined at that point – but it declined much more so when doubt about its authorship arose," and

> A general sense of doubt regarding the artistic value of the picture also sapped the conservators' enthusiasm about resolving its technical problems, and the importance of the treatment fell to zero. Today, the partly cleaned painting sits in the studio cupboard. It will eventually get its cautious cleaning of yellowed varnish, but we will leave the over-paint as is. The continued treatment will commence as a low-priority project when time allows. Until 1993 the painting was part of the permanent collections, and its simple but charming appearance pleased visitors. Gone from the scene, it appears not to be missed. It is highly likely that even after treatment the painting will remain in storage.
>
> [15]

But change is coming, and as discussed in Chapter 2.2, a growing number of heritage professionals are realizing and accepting the fact that they are not the ones to "objectively" decide what needs to be preserved, but to provide expert advice. This new role as expert advisor will be just as important, as expert advisors to the public which then really wants to know.

This leads to a final thought about technological innovation in art conservation, and about the goals of art and heritage conservation in general. At a recent ICOMOS conference and workshop, "Thinking and Planning the Future in Heritage Management," held in 2019 in Amsterdam, professionals took a serious look at what cultural heritage professionals always say that their task is, "We want to preserve cultural heritage for the enjoyment and education of future generations," or something to that effect. Cornelius Holtorf discussed the construction of an underwater nuclear waste storage facility in Sweden [16, 17]. It was designed to be safe for 100,000 years. In terms of the safety of the next few generations, this might be good. But considering that human civilization has only been around for, at the most, 10,000 years, and that the Industrial Revolution only started less than 300 years ago, what does designing a facility that will be safe for 100,000 years mean? The same train of thought applies to cultural heritage. In the ICOMOS workshop which was organized by Holtorf [16], this author conducted three Socratic dialogues, in which participants were asked to provide their personal answers to the following questions:

1. Why do you want to preserve cultural heritage?
2. For which future generation(s) do you want to preserve cultural heritage?
3. What do you want to preserve for future generations? (Give a specific example.)

The answers, in particular, to the second question were as surprising as they were refreshing. "Two or three generations" was the answer from several well-known, well-respected, and highly placed participants, with the ultimate reasoning that after two or three generations, no one in further generations of that person's family or friends would have ever had live contact with that person. And the question was raised in a talk by Sarah May as to what gives current heritage professionals the right to tell future generations what their heritage should be, in essence, infantilizing them [16].

These same questions can be posed to the conservation and conservation science world as they make decisions as to which advanced technologies they want to develop, for which objects, and why. In the answer to the why, there should also be more careful consideration for who conservation professionals are actually trying to reach. Contrary to the "trickle-down" theory of most scientists and heritage professionals, most technological innovations will never benefit the small museum and private conservators who can't afford them. And, as discussed in this book, many of these innovations may actually have unintentionally performed a disservice to the general public at least in terms of color and digital technology, that of creating a new reality in the perception of works of art. And finally, it is questionable whether the goal of conservation should be preserving "everything" for up to and longer than a millennium, as found by a recent survey of heritage professionals (see Figs. 1 and 2 in [18]).

The ultimate task for all heritage professionals including conservation scientists, and those funding their research, is therefore to more critically look at what someone calls "innovative technology," and ask if it really is creating something new *and* useful for art conservation, or is it yet another attempt by big boys with their big toys (of which the author could also be accused of being) to squeeze as much research funding out of available resources as possible. The implied conservation code of ethics argument that if one doesn't try it, one will never know, is about the weakest argument one can use to convince funding agencies to fund something which the public cannot even see, perceive, or care about.

Note

1 The colored figures can be accessed via the online Routledge Resource Centre www.resourcecentre.routledge.com/books/978-1-032-10937-4.

References

1. Stephanie Aulsebrook, 'Late Bronze Age Manipulation of Light and Color in Metal', in *Color and Light in Ancient and Medieval Art*, ed. by Chloë N. Duckworth and Anne E. Sassin (London: Routledge, 2018), p. 36.
2. Theo van Leeuwen, *The Language of Color – An Introduction* (London: Routledge, Taylor and Francis Group, 2011), p. 22.
3. Roy S. Berns, 'Color Reproduction', in *Color Science and the Visual Arts – A Guide for Conservators, Creators and the Curious* (Los Angeles: Getty Conservation Institute, 2016), chapter 7, pp. 183–189.

4. Philippe Colantoni, Ruven Pillay, Christian Lahanier and Denis Pitzalis, 'Analysis of Multispectral Images of Paintings', in *Proceedings of 14th European Signal Processing Conference (EUSIPCO 2006)*, September 4–8, Florence (New York: IEEE, 2006).

5. Theo van Leeuwen, *The Language of Color – An Introduction* (London: Routledge, Taylor and Francis Group, 2011), p. 63.

6. M. E. Chevreul, *The Principles of Harmony and Contrast of Colors and Their Application to the Arts*, based on the first English edition of 1854 translated from the first French edition of 1939 (New York: Reinhold Publishing, 1967), p. 105ff.

7. Liselore Tissen, 'Authenticity and Meaningful Futures for Museums: The Role of 3D Printing', *Journal of the Lucas Graduate Conference*, 9 (2021), 94–122. <https://hdl.handle.net/1887/3246803> [accessed 5 May 2023]

8. Roy S. Berns, 'Colour Reproduction', in *Color Science and the Visual Arts – A Guide for Conservators, Creators and the Curious* (Los Angeles: Getty Conservation Institute, 2016), p. 194.

9. Hans-Christoph von Imhoff, 'Paintings – Their Physical Condition – Their – Perception – Their Interpretation and the Role of the Conservator-Restorer', in *Newsletter Theory and History of Conservation-Restoration, ICOM-CC Working Group* (Paris: International Congress of Museums, 2007), No. 13, pp. 7–9.

10. Louise Lawson and Simon Cane, 'Do Conservators Dream of Electric Sheep? Replicas and Replication', *Studies in Conservation*, 61.suppl 2 (2016), 109–113.

11. Mady Elias, Nadejda Mas and Pascal Cotte, 'Review of Several Optical Non-Destructive Analyses of an Easel Painting. Complementarity and Crosschecking of the Results', *Journal of Cultural Heritage*, 12.4 (2011), 335–345.

12. Kate Seymour, 'Laser Trials at Art Innovation: Three Case Studies', *Cr*, 3 (2003), 24–35.

13. W. Wei, I. Joosten, K. Keim, H. Douna, W. Mekking, M. Reuss and J. Wagemakers, 'Experience with Dust Measurements in Three Dutch Museums', *ZKK – Zeitschrift für Kunsttechnologie und Konservierung*, 21.2 (2007), 261–269.

14. Ricardo Bernárdez-Vilaboa, 'The Implication of Vision and Color in Cultural Heritage', *Heritage*, 3 (2020), 1063–1068.

15. Jørgen Wadum, 'Ravished Images Restored', in *Personal Viewpoints: Thoughts about Paintings Conservation*, ed. by Mark Leonard (Los Angeles: The Getty Conservation Institute, 2003), p. 66.

16. Nour A. Munawar and Helena Rydén, 'Thinking and Planning the Future in Heritage Management', *Conference Report, ICOMOS University Forum*, June 11–14, 2019, Amsterdam. <https://lnu.diva-portal.org/smash/record.jsf?aq2=%5B%5B% 5D%5D&c=73&af=%5B%5D&searchType=LIST_LATEST&sortOrder2=title_ sort_asc&language=sv&pid=diva2%3A1368435&aq=%5B%5B%5D%5D&sf=al l&aqe=%5B%5D&sortOrder=author_sort_asc&onlyFullText=false&noOfRows= 50&dswid=3077> [accessed 5 May 2023].

17. Cornelius Holtorf and Anders Högberg, 'What Lies Ahead? Nuclear Waste as Cultural Heritage of the Future', in *Cultural Heritage and the Future*, ed. by Cornelius Holtorf and Anders Högberg (London: Routledge, 2021), pp. 144–158.

18. Nancy Bell, May Cassar and Matija Strlič, 'Evidence for Informed Preservation Planning and Advocacy: A Synoptic View', *Studies in Conservation*, 63.S1 (2018), S8–S14 (p. S11).

Index

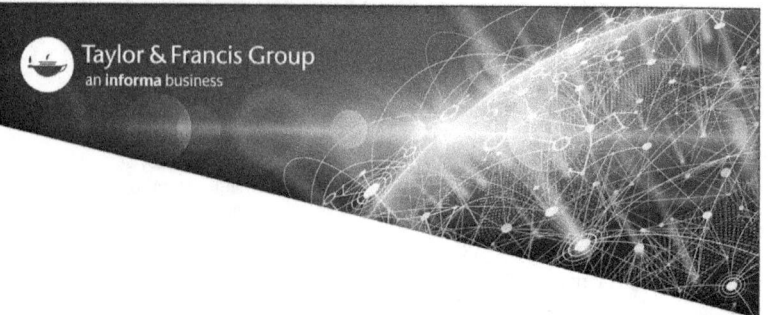
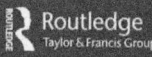
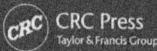

For Product Safety Concerns and Information please contact our EU
representative GPSR@taylorandfrancis.com
Taylor & Francis Verlag GmbH, Kaufingerstraße 24, 80331 München, Germany